Southern Africa's Blue Economy

T0386333

Southern Africa's maritime interests are considerable: its oceans and ports are essential to the wealth of the region, are crucial for trade and are an important source of employment, food and energy. However, regional governments do not pay sufficient attention to the Blue Economy and its potential to stimulate economic growth. Of the 17 UN Sustainable Development Goals, goal Number 14 (Life Below Water) is the least funded. Less than 1% of Official Development Assistance goes toward this goal, and even private investment and funding from philanthropic organizations is grossly inadequate to meet Africa's blue economy needs. It is vital for the international community to face up to the challenges of Africa's Blue Economy and start working on solutions and for southern Africa's Blue Economy policies and goals to be expanded. Just as sustainable development green initiatives show promise, so too could Blue Economy projects and activities.

Southern Africa's rich coastal and marine resources need to be managed on both a national and regional level if they are to be used in a long-term, sustainable way. This book provides, for the first time, a concise study of the constraints and opportunities that the Blue Economy offers for southern Africa and the role that the Southern African Development Community (SADC) could play in fostering a sustainable use of its ocean and coastal resources.

Donald L. Sparks, PhD, is Director of the Distinguished Scholars Program and Emeritus Professor of International Economics at the Citadel (Charleston, South Carolina) and Visiting Professor of International Economics at the Management Center Innsbruck (Austria). He served as a staff assistant to US Senator Ernest Hollings and later senior economist for the South Carolina Sea Grant Consortium where he directed their Indian Ocean Initiative. Prior to that he was the regional economist for Africa in the US Department of State's Office of Economic Analysis. He has received Fulbright awards at SOAS University of London, the National University of Laos, the University of Maribor in Slovenia, the University of Swaziland (now Eswatini), and at the African Union Commission in Addis Ababa, Ethiopia.

Europa Introduction to...

The Focus titles in this series build on the unparalleled worldwide coverage of The Europa World Year Book and its associated regional surveys: Africa South of the Sahara; Central and South-Eastern Europe; Eastern Europe, Russia and Central Asia; The Far East and Australasia; The Middle East and North Africa; South America, Central America and the Caribbean; South Asia; The USA and Canada; and Western Europe, also available online at www.europa-world.com. Books in the series provide students, postgraduates, academics, professionals and researchers with up-to-date, balanced, authoritative and concise introductions to topics in the Europa core areas of country-specific contemporary politics and economics, and regional and international affairs. Volumes in the series, authored by experts, present a factual overview in a concise format, offering readers the opportunity rapidly to research current issues.

Italy's Contemporary Politics
James L. Newell

Economic Transformation in Sub-Saharan Africa
The Way Forward
Donald L. Sparks

China's Belt and Road Initiative at Ten
Country Experiences in the Americas, Oceania and Asia
Robert E. Looney

Southern Africa's Blue Economy
Regional Cooperation for Sustained Development
Donald L. Sparks

Southern Africa's Blue Economy

Regional Cooperation for Sustained Development

Donald L. Sparks

Routledge
Taylor & Francis Group

LONDON AND NEW YORK

First published 2023
by Routledge
4 Park Square, Milton Park, Abingdon, Oxon OX14 4RN

and by Routledge
605 Third Avenue, New York, NY 10158

Routledge is an imprint of the Taylor & Francis Group, an informa business

British Library Cataloguing in Publication Data
A catalogue record for this book is available from the British Library

Library of Congress Cataloging-in-Publication Data
A catalog record has been requested for this book

ISBN: 978-1-032-15614-9 (hbk)
ISBN: 978-1-032-15654-5 (pbk)
ISBN: 978-1-003-24517-9 (ebk)

DOI: 10.4324/9781003245179

Typeset in Times New Roman
by Taylor & Francis Books

Contents

Illustrations

Figures

Tables

Acknowledgements

I would like to thank the School of Oriental and African Studies (SOAS University of London) for hosting me during my Fulbright research grant in the winter term of 2022. That grant gave me the opportunity to conduct research at a number of institutions in London and to organize a symposium, "Africa's Blue Economy: Regional Cooperation for a Sustainable Future". The symposium was attended by over 400 people from around the world and was co-hosted by the Department of Economics and the Centre for Global Finance at the School of Oriental & African Studies, London, the Royal African Society and the Blue Economy Research Institute of the University of Seychelles.

Several participants of the symposium gave me invaluable insights into the challenges that southern Africa faces in developing its blue economy. They are: Dr Elisa Van Waeyenberge, Co-Chair, Department of Economics, SOAS University of London; Dr Nick Westcott Director, Royal African Society; Ms Sylvanna Antat, Director, Blue Economy Research Institute, University of Seychelles; Dr. Louis Rene Peter Larose, Former Minister of Finance, Trade and Economic Planning of the Republic of Seychelles; Dr Nicholas Hardman-Mountford Director, Oceans & Natural Resources, Commonwealth Secretariat, London; Professor Francis Mkwaijande, Senior Lecturer, Mzumbe University, Tanzania and Dr Victor Murinde, Director, Centre for Global Finance, SOAS University of London.

In addition, I learned from many valued colleagues, especially those who contributed to my earlier book on Africa's Blue Economy. Viv Forbes, Kelly Hoareau, and Charlie Colgan have been invaluable colleagues.

Special thanks also go to Cathy Hartley and Iain Frame of the editorial staff at Routledge for their able assistance.

The Blue Economy in southern Africa has become increasingly important as coastal states look at finding ways to strengthen their economies for improved livelihoods as well as to maintain safeguards for their fragile coastal and marine environments. I hope that in some small way this volume will move the discussions forward in a positive manner.

Donald L Sparks, PhD
Seefeld in Tirol, Austria

About the Author

Donald L. Sparks, PhD, is Director of the Distinguished Scholars Program and Emeritus Professor of International Economics at the Citadel (Charleston, South Carolina) and Visiting Professor of International Economics at the Management Center Innsbruck (Austria). He served as a staff assistant to US Senator Ernest Hollings and later was senior economist for the South Carolina Sea Grant Consortium where he directed their Indian Ocean Initiative. Prior to that he was the regional economist for Africa in the US Department of State's Office of Economic Analysis. He has received Fulbright awards at SOAS University of London, the National University of Laos, the University of Maribor in Slovenia, the University of Swaziland (now Eswatini) and at the African Union Commission in Addis Ababa, Ethiopia. He also chaired the Economics Department at the American University in Cairo for a year.

Dr Sparks has been a consultant writing on African economic issues for the Economist Intelligence Unit, the United Nations Industrial Development Organization and the United Nations Council for Namibia. He organized a National Science Foundation/IUCN workshop in Mauritius on Ocean and Coastal Development and Protection and has written extensively on blue economy issues in the western Indian Ocean, visiting over a dozen states in the region. He edited the 2021 volume, *The Blue Economy in Sub-Saharan Africa: Working for a Sustainable Future.*

Dr Sparks serves on the IUCN Commission on Environmental, Economic and Social Policy. He has written the "Economic Trends" chapter for *Africa South of the Sahara* annually since 1986. He holds a BA from the George Washington University and an MA and PhD from the School of Oriental and African Studies (SOAS). Don and his wife live in Charleston, South Carolina, USA and Seefeld in Tirol, Austria.

List of Abbreviations and Acronyms

AfCFT	African Continental Free Trade Area
AfDB	African Development Bank
AIMS	Africa's Integrated Maritime Strategy
AMD	Africa's Maritime Domain
AMTC	African Maritime Transport Charter
AU	African Union
AUC	African Union Commission
AUMSA	African Union Maritime Safety Agency
BBNJ	Biological Diversity of Areas Beyond National Jurisdiction
CADSP	Common African Defense and Security Policy
CEMZA	Combined Exclusive Maritime Zone of Africa
CHANS	Chiefs of African Navies and/or Coast Guards
COMESA	Common Market for East and Southern Africa
CMPT	Comprehensive Maritime Transport Policy
CRESMAC	Coordination of Regional Center for the Maritime Security of Central African States
ECA	East African Community
EEZ	Exclusive Economic Zone
GDP	Gross Domestic Product
IBP	Industrial benefits Policy
ICAM	Integrated Coastal Area Management Plan
IMO	United Nations International Maritime Organization
IOC	Indian Ocean Commission
IORA	Indian Ocean Rim Association
IUU	Illegal, Unreported and Unregulated Fishing
MOWCA	Maritime Organization of West and Central Africa
PMAESA	Ports management Association for Eastern and Southern Africa
PPP	Public Private Partnership

REC	Regional Economic Community
RFMO	Regional Fisheries Management Organizations
SACU	Southern African Customs Union
SADC	Southern African Development Community
SADCC	Southern African Development Coordination Conference
SDG	United Nations Sustainable Development Goal
SIDS	Small Island Developing States
SISR	SADC Industrialization Strategy Roadmap
UNFAO	Food and Agriculture Organization of the United Nations
UNECA	United Nations Economic Commission for Africa
UNEP	United Nations Environment Programme
UNLOS	United Nations Convention on the Law of the Seas

Foreword

The sea is our lifeblood. For Seychelles, our waters have defined us as a nation and as a people. The ocean has helped shape our history, our culture, our economy, our society and our way of life. It has determined what we eat, what we earn and how we live. We understand that our ocean waters are generous but sensitive.

Seychelles has an Exclusive Economic Zone of 1.4 million square kilometers. With such abundant waters come important responsibilities. Because the ocean is so vital to our nation's livelihood, we have taken unprecedented steps to ensure that our children's and their children's future will be able to enjoy our beautiful beaches, our plentiful seafood and a way of life that doesn't take for granted such privileges.

In 2015 we established a Department of Blue Economy whose mandate was to help find the adaptive measures that are required to make the transition from business as usual to a more sustainable use of our marine resources.

In 2018 we adopted our *Blue Economy Roadmap* with the aim of increasing the contribution of our blue resources to ensure economic growth, social, environmental and cultural well-being of our people. It is focused on four key posts: economic diversification and resilience; shared prosperity (creating new jobs and investment opportunities in ocean sectors); food security and integrity of habitats and ecosystem services, sustainable use, and climate resilience. The roadmap hopes to lessen threats such as illegal fishing, marine pollution and the effects of climate change.

As noted in this book, in 2016 we issued the world's first blue bonds, an innovative financing tool for coastal and marine resources which will go towards improving the governance of fisheries and expanding Marine Protected Areas. In 2018 we issued a second blue bond which raised US$ 15 million from international investors that will go towards the expansion of our MPAs.

This book provides an outstanding overview of the challenges and opportunities facing southern Africa's ocean resources. It provides an assessment of the region's blue economy assets and offers insights into how these resources may be better managed in the future. It offers ideas especially on how SADC might harness regional cooperation to foster sustainable regional development.

Indeed, in this important volume, Professor Sparks argues that while some countries such as ours are doing essential work in fostering a sustainable ocean-based blue economy, it is vital that the region works in a more cooperative manner to fight the problems that have no national borders. He makes the important argument that, "To succeed, each country must chart a course that is appropriate to its development ambitions, but it is essential that efforts be completed in a regionally coordinated manner. Should the region decide to take the path that is suggested here, it will take determined efforts at all levels of society. Such efforts will be richly rewarded in a region whose blue economy can lay the foundation for sustainable growth."

Here in Seychelles we welcome such cooperation. For example, earlier this year we met with the leaders of Kenya and spoke about future collaboration in the blue economy including maritime security, military exchanges, agriculture and tourism. I look forward to joining our SADC partners in finding new and creative ways to ensure a sustainable economy and richer life for the next generation. This book provides some interesting and innovative suggestions on how we might move forward. I urge my colleagues in our region – and elsewhere – to consider the ideas found here.

Wavel Ramkalawan
President, Republic of Seychelles

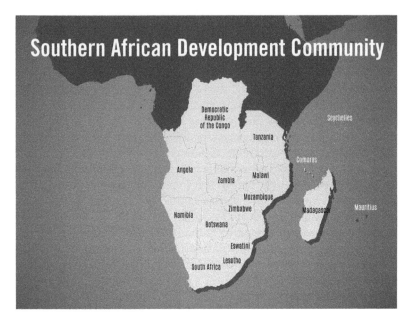

Figure 0.1 Map of the Southern African Development Community
Source: Shutterstock.com

1   Introduction

The sea is inherent to the interesting and complex history of southern and eastern Africa.[1] Maritime interaction with the rest of the world contributed to forging the unique maritime culture of the region and influenced its socio-economic character over a long period of time. Southern Africa's access to the sea and its own wealth made it both receptive and vulnerable to what the sea brought. Since ancient times, the contact with Arabian and Eastern civilizations, Europe and beyond, influenced the region's economic, social and political history.

Southern Africa's initial commercial and coastal partnerships were linked to a thirst for gold, ivory and slaves. Over time it evolved into a complex and prosperous maritime trade and extensive social-cultural interaction, which eventually made way for resistance and colonial conquest. During the second half of the twentieth century this was followed by nationalism, triumph, freedom and realignment. In an environment characterized by a quest for raw materials, the region had to re-establish its political and commercial relationship with the rest of world.

Southern Africa's maritime interests are considerable: its oceans and ports are essential to the wealth of the region, are crucial for trade and are an important source of food and energy. However, regional governments do not place sufficient attention on the blue economy and its potential to stimulate economic growth, poverty reduction and sustained development. The lesson of how important southern Africa's close historical association with the oceans was should be studied by academics, policy makers and the business world. The region's maritime legacy must be reinforced with strong international and regional commercial cooperation, good governance, environmental care, maritime security and sound business approaches to contribute to collectively chart a sustainable development course for the region.

In 2021 UN Secretary-General António Guterres said that year's Intergovernmental Panel on Climate Change (IPCC) report was '…a

DOI: 10.4324/9781003245179-1

code red for humanity. The alarm bells are deafening, and the evidence is irrefutable'.[2] It is clear to all that the planet is in a climate crisis, but what it is less well known is that there is also an oceans crisis. In particular, southern Africa faces devastating consequences if it does not implement sustainable blue economic policies very soon.

When we see clear cutting of forests or strip mining of large areas, most of us want a call to action. Many of us feel that these activities are not sustainable and support policies to restrict them. Unfortunately, equally disturbing practices take place in the deep seas and most of us are not even aware of them. For example, more than half of all key marine biodiversity areas are not protected; ocean dead zones (areas that lack enough oxygen to support marine life) are rising at an alarming rate, from 400 in 2008 to some 700 in 2019; and less than 2% of national research budgets are allocated for marine science. Africa is losing precious mangrove areas (vital for marine nurseries). The cold Benguela Current that originates in the South Pole and continues up the southwest African coast provides essential nutrients for Namibia's fish. Should that current warm up due to climate change, Namibia's fishing industry will be in jeopardy. Illegal, unreported and unregulated fishing is all too common and most countries in Africa find it hard to enforce their maritime laws.

Of the 17 UN Sustainable Development Goals, goal Number 14 (Life Below Water) is the least funded. Less than 1% of Official Development Assistance (ODA) goes toward this goal, and even private investment and funding from philanthropic organizations is grossly inadequate to meet Africa's blue economy needs. It is vital that the international community face up to the code red challenges of Africa's blue economy and start working on solutions such as increased use of blue bonds and other innovative financing mechanisms.

Given the high stakes, it is essential that southern Africa's blue economy policies and goals be expanded. Just as sustainable development green initiatives show promise, so too could blue economy projects and activities. It is imperative that all states adopt strategies to achieve enhanced wealth and wellbeing from the oceans in the coming years. Whether blue economy outcomes will live up to their promise is another matter. There is little doubt that short term gains will be made including from, for example, increased aquaculture and advances in fishing technologies. Yet the long-term sustainability of these endeavors will require concerted effort and significant political will. Finally, as many of the challenges such as marine pollution or maritime security respect no borders, African countries will have to find more ways to boost regional cooperation to find solutions.

Southern Africa has vast coastal and marine resources. These resources will need to be managed on both a national and regional level if they are to be used in a long-term, sustainable way. This book will provide, for the first time, a study of the constraints and opportunities the blue economy offers for southern Africa and what role the Southern African Development Community (SADC) has in fostering a sustainable use of its ocean and coastal resources.

The World Bank defines the blue economy as one that tries '... to promote economic growth, social inclusion, and the preservation or improvement of livelihoods while at the same time ensuring environmental sustainability of the oceans and coastal areas.'[3] The concept came from the 2012 Rio+20 Conference that concluded that heathy ocean ecosystems maker for healthier economies.[4] The blue economy shows much promise, including finding ways to pursue a low carbon path of economic development that would include creating employment opportunities and reducing poverty. Indeed, the World Bank believes that 'Blue growth, or environmentally sustainable economic growth based on the oceans, is a strategy of sustaining economic growth and job creation necessary to reduce poverty in the face of worsening resource constraints and climate crisis.'[5]

Until recently few countries paid much attention to protecting their natural resources. With the publication of Rachel Carson's *Silent Spring* [6] in the 1960s more and more people became aware of the fragility of the planet's ecosystem and in a few short years a 'green economy' movement became almost mainstream. Like land-based resources, marine resources were also thought to be exploitable, virtually unlimited and that there was no need to plan for the future. However, by the beginning of the new millennium there was also a growing awareness of the fragility of the seas and Gunter Pauli's book *The Blue Economy* precipitated a further shift.[7] While their goals and techniques may differ, in many ways both the 'green economy' and the 'blue economy' movements have the theme of sustainability in common. The full implementation of the United Nations Convention on the Law of the Sea (UNCLOS) and related instruments in 1982 was an important step towards ensuring the sustainable development of the world's oceans.

Considerations of the Blue Economy are now becoming more mainstream. In 2017 the United Nations Ocean Conference was focused on finding ways to implement the UN's Sustainable Development Goal #14 ('Life Below Water', as noted in the Appendix). That goal appeals to all nations 'to conserve and sustainably use the oceans, seas and marine resources for sustainable development'.[8]

Interest in Africa's[9] blue economy from academics, government, international organizations and business has grown even more in the past few years. In 2018 Kenya hosted the first global Sustainable Blue Economy Conference which illustrated the growing importance worldwide of optimizing coastal and marine resources. The blue economy movement was strengthened by the African Union's adoption of the 2050 Africa Integrated Maritime Strategy (AIMS).[10] Indeed, the African Union has correctly called the blue economy the 'new frontier of the African Renaissance'.[11]

Nine of the SADC's members have coasts and the majority of the region's international trade is conducted by sea. Maritime zones under African jurisdiction total some 7.5 million square kilometers with vast potential for off-shore and deep sea mineral exploitation. Clearly coastal and marine resources will play key roles as a source of food, employment, energy and economic development for the foreseeable future.

The emergence of the blue economy as an aspirational development framework for southern Africa has taken place in parallel with its rise on the international stage. Understanding the international ocean governance framework underpinning the sustainable blue economy concept is important when balancing inherent tensions between growth and sustainability perspectives. For blue economic growth to be truly sustainable, its governance must be situated within ecological and social realities, over a range of spatial scales and time frames, with progress regularly assessed and adjustments made, as will be discussed below. Such governance must also include regional cooperation. Socially equitable approaches underpinned by scientific knowledge and embedded within an adaptive and holistic governance framework will have the highest chances of lasting success.

While southern African countries have signed up to UNCLOS, very few have taken the next step of domesticating the framework law into their national policies. Furthermore, few countries are making use of tools such as Marine Spatial Planning (MSP) and Ecosystems Based Management (EBM) to inform their policy making and to advance their blue economic activities. A few island countries such as Mauritius and Seychelles have significantly extended their maritime boundaries based on some provisions of UNCLOS, while others such as South Africa have ambitious blue economy programmes (e.g., Operation Phakisa). The majority of southern African countries are not engaged in exploration or exploitation of resources in their Exclusive Economic Zones (EEZ) or in the community heritage areas, despite having enabling global policies and strategies such as UNCLOS and the 2050 AIMS, and having planning tools such as MSP and EBM at their disposal.

It is possible to significantly grow southern Africa's blue economy if countries fully embrace and domesticate global laws and agreements that give them access to resources in the common heritage areas and in their EEZ. However, the region's blue economy also faces numerous challenges. Until recently, the world's coastal and marine areas have been thought of as limitless resources and places to store our waste. The results have ranged from degraded coastal habitats, marine pollution, negative impacts from man-made climate change and overfishing. According to the UN Food and Agriculture Organization (FAO), some 57% of the world's fish stocks are fully exploited and another 30% are over-exploited.[12] Marine fisheries generally contribute some US\$ 270 billion annually to the world economy, according to the FAO.

There are several recent studies and initiatives from the African Union (AU), the World Bank and the United Nations Economic Commission for Africa (UNECA) that look at the future of the blue economy in sub-Saharan Africa in general and southern Africa specifically.

The African Union cites a number of continental-wide initiatives to move the blue economy objectives forward.[13] Its most important initiative is the *2050 Africa's Integrated Maritime Strategy* (2050 AIMS), which calls for the '… urgent imperative to develop a sustainable 'blue economy' initiative which would be a marine version of the green economy, one that improves African citizens well-being while significantly reducing marine environmental risks as well as ecological biodiversity deficiencies'. Its overall vision is, '… to foster increased wealth-creation from Africa's oceans and seas by developing a sustainable thriving blue economy in a secure and environmentally manner.'[14]

Specifically, the major maritime issues the AIMS identifies are:

1 Diverse illegal activities (including toxic waste dumping and oil discharging, arms, drugs and human trafficking and smuggling and piracy);
2 Exploiting energy resources, environmental protection and conservation and climate change;
3 Innovative research; and,
4 Maritime sector development (job creation, trade, infrastructure, communication and technology and logistics).

In addition, the initiative notes a number of other threats, including transnational maritime crime (such as money laundering and crude oil theft), illegal, unreported and unregulated (IUU) fishing, natural disasters, strategic communications systems, vulnerable legal frameworks and the lack of appropriate navigation and hydrographic surveys.

The 2050 AIMS notes a number of strategic actions planned or already underway, including:

- Inter-Agency/Transnational Cooperation and Coordination on Maritime Safety and Security
- Regional Maritime Operational Centers
- Fisheries and Aquaculture
- Integrated Marine Tourism and Leisure Strategy for Africa
- Integrated Maritime Humas Resources Strategy for the Continent
- Disaster Risk Management
- Handling and Shipment of Hazardous Materials and Dangerous Goods
- Maritime Boundaries/Delineation
- Maritime Governance

Importantly, and directly related to this volume, the AU strategy called for the regional economic communities (RECs) and regional members to coordinate and harmonize maritime policies and strategies.[15]

Another important initiative from the African Union is *Agenda 2063* which sets the strategic goal of economic transformation including specific goals for the Blue and Ocean Economy as goal number 6 (maritime resources and energy) and goal number 7 (ports operations and marine transportation). Other related priorities include sustainable natural resource management, renewal energy and water security.

Other AU initiatives include the 2014 *Policy Framework and Reform Strategy for Fisheries and Aquaculture in Africa*. This will help African governments develop appropriate fisheries and aquaculture policies; the 2016 *African Charter on Maritime Security and Safety and Development in Africa* (the Lome Charter) aims to prevent national and transnational crime such as piracy and all forms of illegal trafficking.

In addition to these continental-wide efforts there are a number of regional initiatives currently underway from SADC, the Indian Ocean Commission (IOC) and the Indian Ocean Rim Association (IORA).

The UNECA suggests a variety of challenges and opportunities for the region.[16] The challenges include rising ocean temperatures and ocean acidification resulting in increased loss of fish stocks and the livelihoods that depend on it. Opportunities include low-carbon technological innovation that shifts mindsets toward a better relationship with the natural world. This would include marine energy development such as wave energy (currently being developed in Cape Verde) and tidal power. The ECA's policy handbook called for mainstreaming climate change and environmental sustainability into realistic national and regional policies; increasing investments in climate information services; strengthen environmentally sustainable infrastructure (e.g., 'green' ports and renewable energy); linking ocean energy with high economic value activities such as tourism; better implementing environmental impact assessments and strategic environmental assessments in the blue economy; enhancing early warning systems to mitigate ocean related risks; enhancing national capacities to better cooperate with international agencies such as the International Union for the Conservation of Nature (IUCN); helping expand and/or initiate marine protected areas; raising awareness of these related issues within the region; helping devise national legislation to promote blue economies in selected countries; creating a national capital accounting system that would allow states to promote sustainable energy (and carbon taxes to help finance); and harmonizing regional and continental approaches within the blue economy context.

In its 2017 blue economy study the World Bank identified pathways that countries could take for future action.[17] While realizing there are national and local priorities that may conflict, the study identified ten common steps which include:

1 More accurately valuing natural resource capital including trade-offs among different blue economy sectors;
2 Invest in (and use of) the best science, data and technology;
3 Countries individually weigh the relative importance of their blue economy sectors to decide priorities;
4 Anticipate and adapt to climate change;
5 New investment techniques including blue bonds, debt-for adaption swaps and other innovative instruments;
6 Fully implement the UN Convention on the Law of the Sea;
7 Include active participation of all societal groups, especially women, young people, indigenous peoples and under-represented groups;
8 Develop coastal and marine spatial plans to guide better decision making for the blue economy;
9 Encouraging the private sector to play a key role; and,

10 Find effective partnerships especially from Small Island Developing
   States and coastal LDCs.

There are a number of specific coastal and marine resource challenges
and opportunities on the horizon for southern Africa. They include,
but are not limited to the following.[18]

Governance and regional cooperation

From a governance perspective, states must work towards integrated
marine policies that facilitate blue growth, and address sustainability
issues to avoid acute and negative cumulative impacts. These policies
must be translated into laws that set standards and provide clear regulatory frameworks for expanded ocean industries. Administrative
structures and decision-making processes must also support sustainability. Such reforms may be possible in more developed well-
resourced states. In many southern African nations, however, the lack
of funding and technical expertise, as well as political will, may
hamper, or at least delay, the achievement of these goals. Further, it is
essential that national efforts be done in a way to complement efforts
in other states.

Energy

The east coast of Africa has emerged as one of the most promising
areas in global energy with large natural gas finds in Mozambique and
Tanzania (with 57 total final consumption (tcf) proven natural gas
reserves from its deep water, offshore region).

However, while exploration has taken place in all SADC coastal
member states. the exact amounts of reserves are unknown for most
countries.

There is no doubt that the offshore oil and gas industry was disrupted by COVID-19 during 2020. Oil prices were (and still are, in
November 2022) volatile. In such turbulent times, there exists a need
to act swiftly in order to keep the business viable, to come back strong
when conditions improve. Companies that invest in new technology
today will be ahead of the competition when the industry recovers.

Marine mineral mining has occurred for many years, with most
commercial ventures focusing on aggregates, diamonds, tin, magnesium, salt, sulfur, gold and heavy minerals. Activities have generally
been confined to the shallow near shore (less than 50 m water depth),
but the industry is evolving and mining in deeper water looks set to

proceed, with phosphate, massive sulphide deposits, manganese nodules and cobalt-rich crusts regarded as potential future prospects. Seabed mining is a relatively small industry with only a fraction of the known deposits of marine minerals.

The blue economy development strategy is timely for the SADC region, which has witnessed significant discoveries of large reserves of oil and natural gas in countries such as Mozambique and Namibia in recent years, indicating a huge potential for exploitation of the resource in the region.

The discovery of huge reserves of natural gas has resulted in the formation of the SADC Inter-State Gas Committee. The committee is charged with ensuring the inclusion and promotion of natural gas into the regional energy mix and facilitation of an increase in universal access to energy as well as industrial development in SADC.

Ports

As a generalization, for southern African port operations, consolidating container handling at the site will improve efficiency and vessel turnaround times. Modified existing terminals and new terminals will result in greater economies of scale, better resources for port deployment and marine services by automating both wharf-side and yard operations and reduce the need for inter-terminal haulage. Infrastructure for intra- and inter-state transportation is required for a smooth, seamless transition of cargo from ship to point of destination and vice versa.

Local restrictions on price increases and the regional need to remain competitive in southern Africa would suggest that shippers are unlikely to have to pay more when cargo operations start at new terminals. Innovations should be piloted for ports – small, medium and large – including next-generation vessel traffic management systems that are able to predict congestion hotspots and assists vessel regional route planning. Remote-controlled vessel pilotage, and a maritime sense-making system to boost port operations by preventing illegal bunkering and optimising anchorage utilisation are among the other innovations. Regional cooperation to harmonize port regulations and requirements would be beneficial.

Commercial shipping and aquatic transport are vital modes of transport for the region. In 2009 the SADC region processed 92 million tonnes of traffic through its primary seaport at Durban, South Africa, and other burgeoning ports along the eastern and western seaboards. By 2027, this traffic is projected to increase to 500 million.

Environment/pollution

As mentioned above, pollution knows no national borders. Some of the key sources of pollution include plastics, miscellaneous litter, wastewater, dredging and dumping and shipping activity All along the region's coastline, raw sewage is allowed to pollute the sea as the sewage treatment plants are outdated or inadequate for the growing coastal populations. The city of Cape Town recently completed a study showing extensive fecal contamination of its coastline.[19] It is vital to understand the impacts of pollutants on regional marine ecosystems in order develop policies to ensure long term sustainability.

Biodiversity and marine parks and protected areas

Here again a regional approach is necessary. There are several national marine parks in southern Africa, including for example Mozambique's Bazaruto Archipelago National Park and in Tanzania, Mafia Island Marine Park and Ranga Coielacanth Marine Park. South Africa has 42 marine protected areas[20] in its EEZ, but there is no regional approach. The need for cross border conservation is urgent.[21]

Tourism

Coastal tourism is an important and growing economic sectors for all of southern Africa. Indeed, it is the major economic sector in Seychelles and Mauritius. The challenge, as a recent task force on sustainable tourism development notes, 'is to mitigate the negative impacts of tourism on the coastal and marine environment in Sub-Saharan Africa' and to enhance nature conservation.[22]

Piracy

As will be discussed later in more detail, maritime piracy is a prime example of where regional cooperation is essential. Although it has declined in recent years, between 2010 and 2011 piracy off the Horn of Africa (mostly Somalia) cost the shipping industry some $7bn annually and between 2006 and 2010 some 60 captured crewmembers were killed. It took regional and international cooperation to eliminate the threat. Now piracy has hit west Africa (Gulf of Guinea) but the potential for further piracy activities, especially off Kenya's coast is notable.

Notes

1 This study includes the states in east and southern Africa, plus the western Indian Ocean. The term 'southern Africa' will include the membership of the Southern African Development Community.
2 Sparks (2022).
3 World Bank (2017, p. vi).
4 Blue Economy Concept Paper. New York: United Nations Department of Economics and Social Affairs, 2014.
5 World Bank (2017, p. 5).
6 Carson (1962). It should be noted that Carson's earlier works were about the oceans. Those included *Under the Sea-Wind* (1941), *The Sea Around Us* (1951) and *The Edge of the Sea* (1955).
7 Pauli (2010, 2017).
8 https://sdgs.un.org/goals/goal14.
9 For this study sub-Saharan Africa comprises the 48 states located south of the Sahara Desert and the term Africa is used as a shorthand.
10 African Union (2012).
11 *For the Launch of the 2015–2025 Decade of African Seas and Oceans and the Celebration of the African Day of the Seas and Oceans on 25 July 2015.* Addis Ababa: African Union, 2015.
12 United Nations Food and Agriculture Organization (2018, p. 12).
13 African Union (2019).
14 African Union (2012).
15 It should be noted that other areas of Africa have begun such efforts, including the Maritime Organization of West and Central Africa's (MOWCA) effort to establish an integrated coast guard function network and the Multinational Center for Coordination of Regional Center for the Maritime Security of Central African States (CRESMAC).
16 United Nations Economic Commission for Africa (2016).
17 World Bank (2017).
18 I would like to acknowledge and thank input from my fellow contributors: Viv Forbes, Erika Techera, Charles Colgan and Nick Hardman-Mountford.
19 City of Cape Town (2022).
20 The International Union for Conservation of Nature (IUCN) defines a marine protected area as a clearly defined geographical space, recognised, dedicated, and managed, through legal or other effective means, to achieve the long-term conservation of nature with associated ecosystem services and cultural values.
21 Francis, Nilsson & Waruinge (2022).
22 International task Force on Sustainable Tourism Development. https://iwlearn.net/resolveuid/e2164b06-5525-4772-b3c5-3229396e46fe.

2 Southern Africa's Blue Economy

The region's blue economy shows much promise, including finding ways to pursue a low carbon path of economic development that would include creating employment opportunities and reducing poverty. However, it also faces numerous challenges. As discussed in chapter 1, until recently, the world's coastal and marine areas have been thought of as limitless resources and places to store our waste. The results have ranged from degraded coastal habitats, marine pollution, negative impacts from man-made climate change and overfishing. According to the UN Food and Agriculture Organization (FAO), some 57% of the world's fish stocks are fully exploited and another 30% are over-exploited.[1] Marine fisheries generally contribute some US$ 270 billion annually to the world economy, according to the FAO. The FAO reports that:

> … the fisheries sector in the SADC Region contributes an average of about 2 percent to the SADC GDP, with total average exports worth of USD152 million and average imports of USD100 million. The sector employs an average of 145 000 people, of which more than a million benefit indirectly.[2]

The coastal states in southern Africa have some 7.5 million square kilometers of exclusive economic zones (EEZ) (see Table 2.1). The major economic activities in the 200 mile EEZ include coastal and marine fisheries (at the artisanal and commercial levels), aquaculture, offshore oil and gas exploration, off-shore and deep sea mineral extraction (including diamonds), marine protection services and ship building and repair, shipping, and energy (tidal, solar, and wave). The United Nations Convention on the Law of the Sea (UNCLOS) recognizes the 200 mile distance from the coastline is referred to as Exclusive the Economic Zone (EEZ) which is the area beyond and adjacent to the territorial sea. Individual states have jurisdictional rights governed by the relevant provisions of this Convention.

DOI: 10.4324/9781003245179-2

Table 2.1 SADC Members Exclusive Economic Zones (km²)

South Africa	1,535,538
Seychelles	1,336,559
Mauritius	1,284,997
Madagascar	1,225,259
Mozambique	578,986
Namibia	564,748
Angola	518,433
Tanzania	241,888
Comoros	163,752
DR Congo	1,606
Botswana	0
Eswatini	0
Lesotho	0
Malawi	0
Zambia	0
Zimbabwe	0
Total	7,451,766

Source: World Atlas 2022.

The area beyond the 200 EEZ is the open ocean, referred to as biological diversity of areas beyond national jurisdiction (BBNJ) and until now relatively unregulated. However, in 2017 the UN began serious negotiations to develop the text of an international legally binding instrument under the UNCLOS on the conservation and sustainable use of marine biological diversity of areas beyond national jurisdiction. Since then, there have been four UN sponsored conferences that have begun drafting protocols to be approved by the UN General Assembly. The fifth session was held in late 2022.[3]

The importance of blue resources varies country by country. Those resources play vital roles in Seychelles, Mauritius, Comoros, South Africa and Namibia, while less so in most other countries. The following provides a brief summary and overview of the blue resources in the SADC coastal states.

Mauritius

Mauritius has made the blue economy the center piece of its economic development strategy with the goal of doubling its contribution to GDP by 2025. Its *Oceans Economy Roadmap* plans to use the untapped ocean resources by sustainably coordinating the use of resources. The country created a new Ministry for Blue Economy, Marine Resources, Fisheries, and Shipping with the authority to coordinate and manage ocean-related activities.[4]

Tourism, largely based on visits to beaches, has become a major component of the economy and is one of the most important sources of foreign exchange; it has become increasingly important with the decline of contributions from sugar and textiles.[5] Arrivals of foreign tourists increased from 27,650 visitors in 1970 to over 1 million by the mid-2010s (and 1.4 million in 2019). The largest source of visitors in 2019 was France (302,038, an increase from 285,371 in 2018), followed by the UK (141,520, down from 151,913 in 2018), Réunion (137,570, down from 138,439 in 2018), Germany (129,100 down from 132,780 in 2018) and South Africa (118, 556, down from 128,097 in 2018).

Traditionally, Air Mauritius maintained an arrangement allowing a monopoly of service with French and British routes (via Air France and British Airways), resulting in higher fares and inflexible rates. In an effort to end this monopoly, the Government allowed Virgin Atlantic to operate an additional two flights a week from the UK to Mauritius. Currently some 18 international airlines service the island, while a new direct service to Turkey resulted in a visitor increase of 247% from that country in 2016. In an effort to accommodate environmental considerations with the higher rates of hotel room occupancy, since 1990 the Government has largely ceased issuing permits to construct new hotels.

The fishery sector employs around 12,000 people and contributes 1.5% to GDP.[6] There are four main types of fisheries in Mauritius: artisanal, sport, banks and tuna. Fish also plays an important role as a source of protein. Mauritius regards the fishing sector as an important part of its economic diversification agenda. In early 2006 Mauritius joined the Food and Agriculture Organization of the UN (FAO)'s South West Indian Ocean Fisheries Commission scheme to increase its oceanic bank fisheries. The programme provides technical assistance for boat repair and maintenance. Vessels from Japan, Taiwan and the Republic of Korea (South Korea) fish in offshore waters and transship 15,000–16,000 metric tons of fish, mostly tuna, every year. Fisheries exports have increased six-fold from the early 1990s and will likely continue to benefit from investment in processing plants, although the area has suffered from over fishing which will likely be a detrimental factor in the medium term.

Mauritius is a regional seafood hub and one of the biggest tuna exporters to the European Union from the African Caribbean and

Pacific (ACP) group of countries. Artisanal fishing provides employment and livelihood to some 2,200 fishermen and their families. Mauritius' main commercial port is in Port Louis (quickly becoming a world class shipping facility) and a smaller one in Port Mathurin services shipping between Rodrigues and Mauritius.

Mauritius has some of the strongest coastal zone protection legislation in the region. Its Ministry of Environment, Solid Waste Management and Climate Change has an Integrated Coastal Zone Management (ICZM) division which is key in protecting the country's coastal environment. The Environment Protection Act (amended 2008) created the Integrated Coastal Zone Management Committee, comprised of stakeholders from Government, parastatal bodies, the private sector, NGOs and local authorities.

Mauritius has been advancing Marine Spatial Planning in port infrastructure, shipping, tourism, seafood, fisheries, aquaculture, underwater cultural heritage and marine renewable energy to strengthen its economic diversification.

Seychelles

Seychelles is a beautiful island group and the economy is heavily dependent on coastal tourism, which accounts for around 60% of the country's GDP, employs almost one-third of the labour force and provides more than 70% of hard currency earnings. In addition, the tourism sector has significant "positive spillovers" into the rest of the economy, boosting demand for ancillary services. However, it has been estimated that more than 60% of gross earnings from tourism leaves the country as payment for imported food and other goods, and by way of remittances to tour operators.

In 2018 Seychelles adopted its *Blue Economy Roadmap* which aims to increase the blue resources contribution to economic growth and social, environmental and cultural well-being.[7] It is focused on four key posts: economic diversification and resilience; shared prosperity (creating new jobs and investment opportunities in ocean sectors); food security; and integrity of habitats and ecosystem services, sustainable use, and climate resilience. The roadmap hopes to lessen threats such as illegal fishing, marine pollution, and climate change effects.

The tourism industry began in 1971 with the opening of Mahé International Airport. In that year there were only 3,175 visitors; by 1981 the number had risen to 60,425. Tourist arrivals remained fairly constant during the mid- and late 1990s at 349,861 in 2017 and 428,000 in 2019.

Although Europe was responsible for most of this growth, its share of the total number of visitors has continued to fall. Tourism growth is now being driven by non-traditional markets with direct flight connections, such as the United Arab Emirates (UAE), the Russian Federation and the People's Republic of China.

Seychelles has developed an extensive network of international air links, and nine international airlines service the nation: Air Seychelles, Air Berlin and Condor Flugdienst (Germany); Emirates Airline and Etihad Airways (UAE); Qatar Airways, Ethiopian Airlines, South African Airways and Turkish Airlines. According to the Seychelles Tourism Board, there are direct links from 18 different foreign cities (including new links with Doha, Qatar, and Dubai, UAE), and Air Seychelles has direct flights to London (United Kingdom), Frankfurt (Germany), Paris (France), Milan and Rome (Italy), Johannesburg (South Africa), Bangkok (Thailand) and Port Louis (Mauritius). In 2011 Transaero began a direct air service to Russia and Blue Panorama to Italy, which followed Etihad's entry in 2010. Charter flights, which had been discouraged previously, are now welcome.

The Government estimated the islands' maximum tourist capacity, without detriment to the environment, at 200,000 visitors annually (although this figure has now been exceeded). It was hoped to attract an increasing proportion of visitors interested in the ecological aspects of the archipelago, and to this end attention was focused in the late 1990s on the tourism potential of the outlying islands.

The fishery sector in Seychelles has three main components: artisanal, semi-industrial and industrial, which is made up of the foreign owned purse seiners and long-liners with license to operate in the Seychelles EEZ.[8] Port Victoria is a significant regional tuna transshipment port for these purse seiners, both foreign and Seychelles-flagged vessels.

Seychelles has yet to develop an off-shore energy extractive sector and does not produce oil, gas or minerals, although international companies are exploring for petroleum offshore. It should be noted that Seychelles plans that renewable sources (mostly wind and solar) will contribute at least 15% of energy needs by 2030. There are eight recently installed windmills generating about 2.5% of the total demand on reclaimed coastal land.

In 2016 Seychelles issued the world's first blue bond, an innovative financing tool (debt-for-nature conversion instrument) for coastal and marine resources which will go towards improved governance of fisheries, and expanding Marine Protected Areas (MPAs, or areas set aside to protect marine ecosystems). In 2018 it issued a second blue bond which raised US$ 15 million from international investors, which will go towards improved governance of fisheries and expansion of MPAs. The blue bond is a which purchased $21 million of Seychelles' sovereign debt to refinance it under more favorable terms. A portion of repayments will go to fund climate change adaptation, sustainable fisheries, and marine conservation.

Namibia

Owing to the cold, nutrient-rich Benguela Current (as noted above), Namibia's 1,500 km of coast is one of the richest fishing areas in the world. Indeed, the country is Africa's primary exporter of fish and fish products, and the industry currently employs some 24,000 workers (of whom 43% are seagoing personnel and 57% are engaged in onshore processing) and contributes approximately 3.5% of the country's GDP. Fisheries provides about 16,800 jobs directly making this sector the second most important export earner after mining.[9]

Prior to independence from South Africa, however, Namibia received no tax or licence fees from fishing because the illegal occupation of the territory deprived it of an internationally recognized fishing zone within the usual limit of 200 nautical miles (370 km). The inshore fishery, for pilchard, anchovy and rock lobster, is controlled by Namibian and South African companies. Other important species include hake, horse mackerel and crab. Following independence, the Namibian authorities enforced a 370 km exclusive economic zone, thereby achieving considerable success in restocking its overfished waters. Over the past 15 years the Namibian Government has allocated significant funding to the aquaculture sector, but with few demonstrable returns in terms of food security and employment creation.

Diamonds (found along the coast and off shore) form a key component of Namibia's economy. Diamond mining has historically contributed approximately 70% of the sector's GDP and some 10% of national GDP.

A new Diamond Act, to succeed legislation in force since before independence, was approved by the Namibian parliament in mid-1999. The Act allows individuals to apply for licences to trade in, import or export diamonds, subject to criminal penalties for unauthorized dealing. Namibia is co-operating in international efforts to ensure that diamonds from conflict areas are not used to support continued warfare (so-called "conflict diamonds").

In 2007 the Government and De Beers established a 50:50 joint venture, the Namibia Diamond Trading Co, which was to be responsible for sorting, establishing value and marketing Namdeb's output to local firms as well as to the world market. The Government implemented a new marketing agreement in 2010 to allow firms to buy uncut stones direct from Namdeb. This new arrangement was expected to allow local firms to cut more locally mined stones. Indeed, in 2014 LLD Diamonds Namibia opened a large-scale diamond cutting and polishing enterprise in Windhoek. Such upstream activities will help to boost diamonds' share of Namibian GDP.

Namibia has extensive phosphate deposits along its coast. In 2013 the Government issued licences to two firms, LL Namibia Phosphates and Namibian Marine Phosphate. However, also in that year the Government declared an 18-month moratorium on phosphate mining pending the results of an environmental impact study to gauge the risk to marine life and the fishing industry.

Although no commercial petroleum discovery has yet been made, Namibia is believed to have considerable offshore reserves of natural gas, estimated at as much as 560,000m. cu m in the Kudu gas field off !Nami‡Nûs (formerly Lüderitz).

South Africa

South Africa has the largest EEZ in the region with a long coastline that spans the Atlantic Ocean in the west and the Indian Ocean in the east. The Benguela Current of the west coast is one of the most productive ocean ecosystems in the world in terms of biomass production and fishery resources due to the upwelling of cold, nutrient rich water.[10]

South Africa's blue economy supports thousands of jobs and add millions of rand to the national economy, with coastal goods and services estimated to contribute 35% to South Africa's gross domestic product (GDP). About one third of South Africa's population live within 60km of the coast.

In 2014 South Africa launched *Operation Phakisa*, a national development strategy based on blue resources.[11] The plan focuses on six priority areas: marine transport and manufacturing; offshore oil and gas exploration; aquaculture; marine protection services and ocean governance; small harbors; and coastal and marine tourism. South Africa's blue economy, according to Operation Phakisa, has the potential to contribute up to R177 billion to South Africa's GDP by 2033 and create between 800,000 and 1 million jobs. Operation Phakisa Initiative 10 "Marine Spatial Planning Process", led by the Department of Environmental Affairs will be an important component in guiding blue economy planning for South Africa.

South Africa's fishing industry (Africa's largest) provides direct employment and income for at least 27,000 people (an indirect employment for another 50,000–100,000), but contributes less than 1% of the country's GDP.[12] The industry has three sub-sets: the commercial/ industrial, recreational and subsistence/artisanal fisheries. Together they go for over 250 marine species (United Nations Food and Agriculture Organization 2018).[13]

The commercial fisheries field consists of about 1,800 vessels and their annual production is around 600,000 tons. The aquaculture sector employs around 15,000 people contributing perhaps R3 billion to the overall economy.

South Africa is home to the region's most developed, efficient and important ports. There are six major ports: Durban, Richards Bay, Port Elizabeth, East London, Cape Town and Saldanha, which also serve the neighboring SADC landlocked countries including Zambia, Zimbabwe, Lesotho, Eswatini and Malawi. Over 30,000 vessels pass through South Africa's ports annually. Besides on and off loading cargo, these ports offer ship repair and other services.

Other important industries include energy and tourism. South Africa's oil and gas industries show potential. There are about 80 oil rigs in the Western Cape. Coastal tourism has the potential to contribute R21,4 billion to GDP and create 116,000 jobs by 2026, according to the Nairobi Convention.

Comoros

Comoros comprises three volcanic islands: Grande Comore (Ngazidja), Anjouan (Nzwani) and Moheli (Mwali) which form the Union of the Comoros (not including the French overseas department of Mayotte). The Comoros EEZ is an estimated 160,000 km^2 covering 427 km of coastline (about 100 times larger than its land area) and it is surrounded by several other EEZs, including those of France (with its territory of Mayotte), Madagascar, Mozambique, Seychelles and Tanzania.

Comoros' economy is dependent on its blue resources. According to the UNDP's Regional Seas Programme, the Comoros' annual economic output from the ocean was valued at US$ 0.2 billion, or 18% of the Comoros' GDP of US$ 0.7 billion.[14]

Fisheries (mostly local artisanal fishers) contribute about 30% to the ocean economy and its coastal communities depend on fishing for income and food security. Tuna is the most valuable fish caught there. Its annual catch is estimated at 33,000 MT/year. Domestic fishery production in Comoros has been reported as approximately 20,000

MT/year in several reports over the last decade. Large pelagic sharks are also found in its EEZ.

Besides fish other resources include octopus, shrimp, shells and oysters for consumption, and oyster shells, sand and corals for construction. The country has only one deep water port, on the island of Anjouan. While Comoros has no proven oil and gas reserves, there has been exploration in the Mozambique Channel and it is exploring renewable energy resources including solar and wind.

Comoros has a beautiful coastal natural environment and the potential to become an important tourism destination. However, despite these strong tourism assets, it currently has relatively few tourist arrivals, primarily due to its remote location, political uncertainty and inadequate tourism infrastructure.

Angola and the Democratic Republic of Congo

Angola and the Democratic Republic of Congo (DRC) provide an interesting dilemma regarding their blue resources. For Angola, oil is the country's most valuable resource, accounting for some 40% of GDP and 75% of government revenues. Much of this oil is found off-shore in its enclave of Cabinda, which is separated from the rest of Angola by the DRC at the mouth of the Congo River. The DRC does not have much oil production (only a few minor fields) and has yet to explore potential reserves off-shore or inland.

However, under the UNCLOS (that governs which strips of sea belong to which countries), the DRC could claim some large oil fields currently held in Cabinda. Those reserves, which are responsible for about half of Angola's production, are in Congolese waters.

In 2014 the two countries signed the Joint Interest Zone (JIZ) which agreed on maritime rights and resources, but the DRC was under extreme financial pressure at the time and made concessions to Angola.

In 2009 the DRC passed legislation regarding its claims to the oil fields but the legislation never went into force. According to Edmond, et al, "...there is little chance the DRC will ever take control of its maritime territory as defined under international law or even reach a fair compromise. Its dependence on its neighbour makes the prospect of upsetting Angola too risky".[15]

Mozambique

Mozambique has the third longest coastline in Africa (hosting 10 ports), and its blue resources make important contributions to its economy.[16] In 2009, the fisheries and aquaculture sector in Mozambique contributed to 1.6 per cent of GDP, although its fisheries potential is much larger, with a potential yield of 220,000 and 330,000 tonnes. Mozambique has pristine beaches and its coastal tourism sector provides some 3.2 per cent to GDP and employs more than 350,000 people.

Mozambique's fisheries sector is composed of artisanal fishers mainly of small pelagic fish (representing over 90% of the catch). The semi-industrial fishing sector employs over 400,000 people and accounts for 93% of the country's total marine fish catch.

Aquaculture and mariculture are small industries and employ about 2,000 people in commercial seaweed farming (80% of whom are women), and less than 1,000 people in commercial prawn farming.

Mozambique mines coal. aluminum, titanium, zircon and rutile (an oxide mineral composed of titanium dioxide and used in porcelain and glass manufacturing) from coastal sand dunes. Mozambique produces limited amounts of oil and biofuels.

Tanzania

Tanzania's coastal resources are important for many economic sectors including fishing, shipping, tourism, aquaculture and related industries. Nearly 16 million people rely on coastal resources for their livelihood and fish makes up nearly 20% of the country's animal protein intake.[17]

Tanzania has some of the world's richest fishing grounds, according to global species database FishBase.[18] Of these, about 50 are commercially important. Over 180,000 people are employed in the fisheries sector (most from small-scale fisheries), with a further 19,223 people involved in fish farming.

Tanzania has a variety of fish stocks with more than 1,700 species (most important of which are tuna, bream, parrot fish, sharks, rays, swordfish, prawns, grouper, snapper and octopus). The mariculture industry comprises mostly shrimp farms, seaweed and shellfish culture. Coral reefs are important for most of Tanzania's artisanal fish production.

Dar es Salaam is the country's major port with a capacity of 10.1m tonnes per year. The port handles over 92% of the country's maritime port's trade. The port also is important for the landlocked states of Malawi, Zambia, Democratic Republic of Congo, Rwanda, Burundi and Uganda.

Tanzania produces natural gas, mainly from the off-shore Songosongo and Mtwara regions. Recent natural gas exploration in Cabo

Delgado in the country's north are the largest finds in some two decades

Madagascar

Madagascar has 5,603 km of coastline and its blue resources are vital for food security, especially for those who live along the coast. Indeed, fishing is one of the main means of subsistence for the coastal communities. The industrial seine and longline fisheries are centered around tuna. Official fisheries statistics indicate catches of 10,000 to 11,000 tonnes per year.[19]

Aquaculture farms are becoming increasingly important and include recently producing environmentally sustainable sea cucumber. Seaweed farming also has the potential for increased production.

Madagascar has six international ports: Toamasina, Mahajanga, Antsiranana, Nosy-be, Toliara and Ehoala, and 12 ports for coastal navigation: Vohémar, Maroantsetra, Mananjary, Manakara, Taolagnaro, Morombe, Morondava, Maintirano, Port Louis, Antsohihy, Sambava and Antalaha.

Notes

1 United Nations Food and Agriculture Organization (2018, p. 12).
2 http://www.fao.org/africa/news/detail-news/en/c/459962/.
3 https://www.un.org/bbnj/.
4 Mauritius Blue Economy, Nairobi Convention Secretariat, Country Profile. https://www.nairobiconvention.org/mauritius-country-profile/ocean-economy-mauritius-country-profile/.
5 Much of this section is sourced from "Seychelles: Economy", in *Africa South of the Sahara 2018* (47th Edition) London: Routledge, Taylor and Francis Group, 2020, pp. 1074–1077.
6 Economic Development Board. 2019. Fishing, Seafood and Aquaculture: https://www.edbmauritius.org/opportunities/ocean-economy/fishing-seafood-and-aquaculture/.
7 Sahuque (2015).
8 *African Development Bank. Seychelles Country Report 2014. African Development Bank Group. 2014.*https://www.afdb.org/fileadmin/uploads/afdb/Documents/Generic-Documents/Eastern_Africa%E2%80%99s_Manufacturing_Sector_-_Promoting_Technology__Innovation.pdf.
9 Much of this section is sourced from "Namibia: Economy", in *Africa South of the Sahara 2018* (47th Edition) London: Routledge, Taylor and Francis Group, 2020, pp. 890–895.
10 Cochrane et al. (2009).
11 https://www.operationphakisa.gov.za/Pages/Home.aspx.
12 United Nations Food and Agriculture Organization (2018).

13 South Africa Ocean Economy, Nairobi Convention Secretariat, https://www.nairobiconvention.org/south-africa-country-profile/south-africa-ocean-economy-2/.
14 https://www.nairobiconvention.org/comoros-country-profile/comoros-ocean-economy/.
15 Edmond et al. (2019).
16 Fishery and Aquaculture Country Profiles. Mozambique (2019). Country Profile Fact Sheets. https://www.fao.org/fishery/.
17 https://www.nairobiconvention.org/tanzania-country-profile/tanzania-ocean-economy-2/.
18 https://www.fishbase.se/country/CountryChecklist.php?vhabitat=saltwater&c_code=834.
19 https://www.nairobiconvention.org/madagascar-country-profile/madagascar-ocean-economy-2/.

3   A Brief History of the Southern African Development Community and Blue Economy Challenges

SADC originated in the 1960s and 1970s when the region's majority-ruled countries (the so-called Frontline States) and liberation movements were working toward ending minority-ruled South Africa's apartheid system of government.[1] In 1979 nine southern African neighbors –Angola, Botswana, Lesotho, Malawi, Mozambique, Eswatini (Swaziland), Tanzania, Zambia and Zimbabwe – signed the Lusaka Declaration (*Southern Africa: Toward Economic Liberation*) which created the Southern African Development Coordination Conference (SADCC) the following year, in 1980. In 1992 the member states transformed the institution into SADC (see Table 3.1).

SADC has 25 legally binding protocols dealing with issues such as defense, economic development, illicit drug trade, free trade and movement of people. The following is a list of SADC Protocols and dates signed:

- Protocol Against Corruption (2001)
- Protocol on Combating Illicit Drug Trafficking (1996)
- Protocol on the Control of firearms Ammunition and other Related Materials (2001)
- Protocol on Culture, Information and Sport (2001)
- Protocol on Education and Training (1997)
- Protocol on Energy (1996)
- Protocol on Extradition (2002)
- Protocol on the Facilitation and Movement of Persons (2005)
- Protocol on Finance and Investment (2006)
- Protocol on Fisheries (2001)
- Protocol on Forestry (2002)
- Protocol on Gender and Development (2008)
- Protocol on Health (1999)
- Protocol to the Treaty Establishing SADC on Immunities and Privileges (1992)

DOI: 10.4324/9781003245179-3

- Protocol on Legal Affairs (2000)
- Protocol on Mining (1997)
- Protocol on Mutual Legal Assistance in Criminal Matters (2002)
- Protocol on Politics, Defense and Security Cooperation (2001)
- Protocol on Science, Technology and Innovation (2008)
- Protocol on Shared Watercourses (2000)
- Protocol on the Development of Tourism (1998)
- Protocol on Trade (1996)
- Protocol on Trade in Services (2012)
- Protocol on Transport, Communications and Meteorology (1996)
- Protocol on Tribunal and Rules Thereof (2000).

In order for a protocol to enter into force, two thirds of the member states must ratify it. Any member state that had not initially become party to a protocol can assent to it later.

SADC has not completely followed the classic pattern of regional integration (see Table 3.2). Instead, as mentioned earlier, it started as a regional affiliation to lessen dependency on then apartheid ruled South Africa and has developed into a hybrid integrated regime. For example, it doesn't constitute a common market, although it is a stated goal (again, see Table 3.2). Further, as the timeline suggests, SADC is well behind its efforts to reach an economic union.

Regional economic integration refers to agreements between countries (usually) in a geographic region to reduce tariff and nontariff barriers to the free flow of goods, services and factors of production (including people and capital) between each other.

The most basic form is a Preferential Trade Area (PTA) where the members reduce the tariff barriers between each other but leave their respective external barriers against all other trade partners (for example, US-Canada PTA). A Free Trade Area (FTA) eliminates trade barriers between members but leaves their respective external barriers against all other trade partners (for example NAFTA, now USMCA). A Customs Union adds the requirement that all members set a common trade policy against non-members (for example, the Southern African Customs Union) while a Common Market does the above and adds the free movement of labor and capital and sets a common trade policy against non-members (for example, the former European Common Market). An Economic Union requires members to harmonize their tax, monetary and fiscal policies can include creating a common currency, and generally concedes some sovereignty to the larger organization (for example, the European Union).

Table 3.1 SADC Historical Timeline

1975	Frontline States established (Angola, Botswana, Lesotho, Mozambique, Tanzania, Zambia and Zimbabwe)
1980	Lusaka Declaration launching the Southern African Development Coordination Conference (SADCC) signed by nine states (Angola, Botswana, Lesotho, Malawi, Mozambique, Swaziland – now Eswatini, Tanzania, Zambia and Zimbabwe)
1982	SADC Secretariat headquarters established in Gaborone, Botswana
1990	Namibia joins the SADC
1992	SADC Treaty and Declaration signed at the Windhoek Summit in Namibia, transforming the SADCC into the SADC
1994	South Africa joins the SADC
1995	Mauritius joins the SADC
1998	Democratic Republic of the Congo and Seychelles join the SADC
2000	SADC restructured and the Secretariat moves entirely to Gaborone
2004	The Regional Indicative Strategic Development Plan (RISDP) launched in Arusha, Tanzania
2005	The RISDP and the Strategic Indicative Plan for the Organ (SIPO) initiated
2005	Madagascar joins the SADC
2005	The SADC Tribunal is inaugurated in Windhoek
2006	At the Consultative Conference in Windhoek the SADC and International Cooperating Partners (ICPs) adopt the Windhoek Declaration, a framework for partnership between the SADC and the ICPs
2008	SADC Free Trade Area established

| 2011 | The Desktop Assessment Review of the RISDP is published, reviewing five years of progress in the implementation of the Plan |
| 2017 | Comoros joins the SADC |

Source: SADC Secretariat and the author.

Table 3.2 SADC's stages and goals of regional economic integration

2005	Regional Indicative Strategic Development Plan (RISDP)
2008	Free Trade Area established
2010	Customs Union established
2015	Common Market established
2016	Monetary union
2018	Single currency/Economic union

Source: SADC Secretariat.

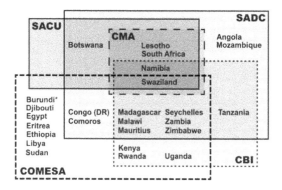

Figure 3.1 Overlapping Memberships in Southern Africa
Source: Compiled by the author

Table 3.3 Intra-SADC Trade (% of total trade that is with members)

		2000	2015
Angola			
	Exports	0.2	4.1
	Imports	7.8*	6.1
Botswana			
	Exports	11.6	29.5
	Imports	80.9	80.7
DRC			
	Exports	1.2	81.5**
	Imports	21.0	46.1**
Lesotho			
	Exports	27.8	78.0**
	Imports	79.6	78.1**
Madagascar			
	Exports	3.1	5.8
	Imports	9.8	10.1
Malawi			
	Exports	11.8	5.4
	Imports	35.3	7.4
Mauritius			
	Exports	1.7	15.7
	Imports	15.8	9.9
Mozambique			
	Exports	55.5	25.8
	Imports	64.0	32.0
Namibia			
	Exports	33.9	54.5
	Imports	87.4	72.1

		2000	2015
Seychelles			
	Exports	3.7	0.5
	Imports	90.4	12.5
South Africa			
	Exports	10.6	23.4
	Imports	1.3	6.1
Swaziland			
	Exports	85.3	81.6
	Imports	94.7	81.2
Tanzania			
	Exports	7.2	10.6
	Imports	13.8	3.6
Zambia			
	Exports	29.3	23.1
	Imports	68.7	52.2
Zimbabwe			
	Exports	82.1	68.6
	Imports	63.6	42.4

Source: SADC Secretariat, 2017.
Notes: * = 2002; ** = 2014.

Regional economic integration can be seen as an attempt to achieve additional gains from the free flow of trade and investment between countries beyond those attainable under international agreements such as the WTO.

The political case for integration has two main points: (1) by linking countries together, making them more dependent on each other, and forming a structure where they regularly have to interact, the likelihood of violent conflict and war will decrease; and, (2) by linking countries together, they have greater clout and are politically much stronger in dealing with other nations.

Complicating SADC's membership is the "spaghetti bowl" effect, with numerous overlapping memberships (see Figure 3.1). Such membership makes it difficult for each member to fully participate in the organization's goals due to capacity constraints.

Since most of SADC members generally produce and export primary products, the scope for large intra-regional trade is limited, at least for now. For most members, intra-regional trade comprises between 6% and 12% of total trade. Botswana, Lesotho, Eswatini and Namibia are the exceptions, although Zimbabwe, Zambia and the DRC have significant intra-regional trade (see Table 3.3).

While economic integration and trade are at the heart of SADC, the organization has also established a range of other blue economy-related initiatives. There a number of sectors where SADC could help implement coordinated regional strategies for a sustainable blue economy, as will be discussed in the next chapter. SADC as already taken the initiative in several sectors. They include the following.

Agriculture and Food Security

SADC's Food, Agriculture and Natural Resources Directorate is responsible for food security, crop and livestock production and fisheries. Of particular relevance here would be aquaculture and mariculture.

Natural Resources

SADC addresses natural resource challenges in forest, wildlife, cross-border conservation areas, water and fisheries. Again, these issues are cross border in nature and require a coordinated regional approach.

Poverty Eradication and Policy Dialogue

There are numerous other socio-economic challenges that contribute to poverty in southern Africa and poverty reduction is SADC's ultimate goal. The SADC Council of Non-Governmental Organizations is the institution in charge of in implementing the "Poverty and Development Programme" with implications for blue economy resources. The SADC region contains ten coastal states with some 7.5 million km^2 of maritime zones (with vast potential for off-shore and deep sea mineral exploitation) and the majority of the region's exports and imports come via sea. Clearly coastal and marine resources will play key roles as a source of food, energy and economic development for the foreseeable future.

Fisheries

The SADC Protocol on Fisheries and its Annex, Statement of Commitment to combat Illegal, Unreported and Unregulated (IUU) fishing by SADC ministers responsible for fisheries is an excellent example of regional cooperation. The SADC Secretariat, in cooperation with the World Wide Fund for Nature (WWF) held a webinar in 2020 entitled "Improving Regional Fisheries Governance and Sustainability through Transparency – focus on West Indian Ocean Tuna Fisheries". The Marine Resource Management Division in South Africa's Department for Environment, Forestry and Fisheries, facilitated the webinar, which was attended by 48 participants representing 11 SADC Member States, and ten partner organisations. Presentations focused on the industrial fishing and small-scale fishing sectors, as well as unregulated fisheries, which are those in areas beyond national jurisdiction.

Maritime Security

The Regional Anti-Piracy Prosecution and Intelligence Coordination Centre (RAPPICC) was opened in Seychelles in 2013. That same year South Africa's President extended the duration of the South African National Defense Force's (SANDF) operation to monitor piracy off Mozambican and Tanzanian coats until March 2014. The successful counter-piracy operations off the coast of northern Somalia may have driven the operations of these groups south. In 2011 South Africa agreed to provide maritime security and prevent piracy with Mozambique and Tanzania in the Mozambique Channel. "Operation Copper" has resulted in a sharp decline of piracy off the southeast African coast. South Africa is now considering shifting resources to the southwest African coast where it has entered into the marine ecosystem convention with Namibia and Angola. While the major threats to maritime security in the Benguela Current are illegal fishing and drug trafficking, the potential threat of piracy further up the West Coast may soon necessitate anti-piracy operations in this area as well.[2]

Energy

There is no doubt that the offshore oil and gas industry was disrupted by COVID-19 during 2020. As mentioned earlier, oil prices remain volatile and storage capacity is limited. In such turbulent times, there exists a need to act swiftly in order to keep the business viable, to come back strong when conditions improve. Companies that invest in new technology today will be ahead of the competition when the industry recovers. Digitalisation of the value chain, also known as value chain optimisation is an essential part of staying competitive.

Marine Mining

Marine mineral mining has occurred for many years, with most commercial ventures focusing on aggregates, diamonds, tin, magnesium, salt, sulfur, gold and heavy minerals. Activities have generally been confined to the shallow near shore (less than 50 m water depth), but the industry is evolving and mining in deeper water looks set to proceed, with phosphate, massive sulphide deposits, manganese nodules and cobalt-rich crusts regarded as potential future prospects. Seabed mining is a relatively small industry with only a fraction of the known deposits of marine minerals.

Ports and Shipping

As previously mentioned, commercial shipping and aquatic transport are vital modes of transport for the region. Total port traffic in Southern Africa will jump from 92 million tonnes in 2009 to 500 million tonnes by 2027 according to SADC. Chapter 8 of *SADC's Protocol on Transport, Communications and Meteorology* encourages its members to better develop port and inland waterway infrastructure throughout Southern Africa. Eventually this should promote an integrated, multimodal transportation sector. Members have agreed to cooperate on a harmonized regional policy for maritime and inland waterway transport, based on the standards and recommended practices of the International Maritime Organisation (IMO). While SADC Member States have acceded to the Status of Convention of the International Maritime Organization, most of them lack the technical capacity to maintain these global standards. Many regional ports operate at or near capacity and suffer delays due to poor integration with other modes of transport and slow clearance by regulatory bodies.

SADC's 2012 *Regional Infrastructure Development Master Plan* identified several water transport challenges facing the region.[3] These include: intermodal management when vehicles in port areas often efficient operations; material handling, as some ports are unable to freight at the docks; customs facilitation as clearing cargo can be delayed for up to two months due to ineffective customs; and location management since most ports in the region lie near densely populated industrial zones that limit potential (and much needed) expansion.

While SADC members have over 60 maritime and inland waterway transport projects in development, they are not being as well coordinated as they could be and they are concentrated on two centers, Dar-es-Salaam in Tanzania and Walvis Bay in Namibia. However, it should be mentioned that in addition developments are also underway at the ports of Nacala, Beira and Maputo in Mozambique, Luanda in Angola and Durban in South Africa.

The private sector has driven most of these projects. Private sector investment in Dar-es-Salaam and Beira ports has been profitable due to their connections to coal mines in Mozambique and copper mines in Zambia. As noted above, these public-private partnerships are essential for SADC's development of maritime and inland waterways.

Notes

1   See Magliveras (2007).
2   Brits & Nel (2016).
3   https://www.sadc.int/files/7513/5293/3530/Regional_Infrastructure_Develop ment_Master_Plan_Executive_Summary.pdf.

4   Conclusion

How the Southern African
Development Community can Foster a
Sustainable Regional Blue Economy

Expanded economic growth and development is promoted by the
business community, economists and politicians; however, rapid
growth clearly is not in the best long-term interest for the planet and
the international community. Our oceans are stressed, coral is dying,
waters are warming due to climate change and species are not reco-
vering from these events, never mind overfishing, and pollution of the
marine environment. We need to value our oceans and understand
them better before we inflict more damage on them. There must be a
balance with what resources are taken from the ocean and utilised and
the need to make a profit solely to benefit a specific business or
industry or particular political agenda at global, regional, national
and local-government level.

Southern Africa has been experiencing a rapid erosion of the asset
base of oceans and inland waters due to overfishing, pollution from
land-based sources, mangrove deforestation, climate change and ocean
acidification. As a result, there is a need for policy changes at the
national and regional levels in order to realize the full potential of the
blue economy. Such policies will have to include responsible and
sustainable approaches that are more environmentally, socially and
economically successful.

The influence of blue economy policies and goals will likely continue to expand. Just as sustainable development initiatives have
flourished, so too will blue economy projects and activities. It is likely
that eventually all SADC states will adopt strategies to achieve
enhanced wealth and wellbeing from the oceans, in the coming years.
Whether blue economy outcomes will live up to their promise is
another matter. There is little doubt that short term gains will be
made including from, for example, increased aquaculture and advances in fishing technologies. Yet the long terms sustainability of these
endeavors will require concerted effort and significant political will.

DOI: 10.4324/9781003245179-4

SADC has a range of integration targets, some of which it has met and some of which it may never reach. As discussed earlier, SADC's success is further imperiled by member states' participation in other regional security schemes that may compete with or could undermine SADC's aims. However, the region has finally recognized this problem, and it is possible that the Tripartite Strategy will result in one very large regional free trade area and at some point reduce such competition.[1] It also should be noted that SADC's record outside the economic sphere has been mixed. For example, according to Human Rights Watch, "SADC has been criticized for its laxity on making human rights compliance within its member states a priority".[2]

It may well be that the traditional linear integration model (ie, starting at a PTA and then evolving into a FTA, CU, CU and EU as discussed above) is not suited to southern Africa.[3] Like regional trade blocs elsewhere, there are inherent conflicts when members have varying degrees of economic development, income, political stability, transportation infrastructure and governing philosophies. South Africa's GDP of $740 billion is almost 300% greater than that of Seychelles (with $2.5 billion), the group's smallest economy.[4] Levels of competency vary, as do levels of education (for example, the literacy rate of Seychelles is 97%, compared to 65% for Malawi). And, as discussed above, the region's output is mostly primary products with limited regional markets.

Another approach (that is more organic) and that may be more appropriate especially for enhancing the blue economy, is the variable geometry (or sometimes called the development integration) approach. This allows much more flexibility and takes into account the various differences noted above. Indeed, this is the model the European Union used when it created its monetary union as initial members could have opted in but were not required to.

Many of the regional challenges (developmental, security, climate, diseases and natural disasters, to name a few) cannot be solved effectively by individual members. Floods and drought know no boundaries. Wars spread across borders. Business now seek low cost production and customers often without regard to nationalities. Southern Africa certainly needs increased regional cooperation. In that regard, the important question remains about how deep and wide should – and could – the community become?

The question of how wide is probably easier to answer. Given that membership in existing regional organizations (e.g. COMEAS or ECA) show little interest in leaving, they are unlikely to jump ship for SADC. The political and economic costs of such a move could be considerable, while the gains (at least in the short term) could be hard to measure. Officially SADC does not seek to add more members, although Burundi has applied and Rwanda has expressed interest. And should the Common Market for COMESA-EAC-SADC ever become truly effective, then the idea of expansion would be answered by default.

The question of deeper integration is harder to resolve. As noted above, the group is in the process now of the harmonization in a range of areas (even sports, for example, with the organization hosting its own multi-sport event, the SADC Games, which was first held in 2004 in Maputo and the seventh last year in Luanda). Again, a strengthened and successful Tripartite grouping would necessitate wider harmonization.

Nonetheless, there are areas for deeper harmonization and cooperation, as this volume argues. Perhaps the most obvious, and one of the most important one is in the area of the blue economy.

In April 2022 SADC and the African Development Bank introduced a US$ 9.2 million "Programme for Improving Fisheries Governance and Blue Economy Trade Corridors" (known as ProFishBlue) in the SADC area. ProFishBlue will support best practices of fisheries governance and blue economy trade corridors in the SADC region. The project, "… aims to promote sustainable management of fisheries resources within the blue economy context to improve food and nutritional security, create employment through value chain activities, facilitate intra-regional trade, and build adaptive capacity". It comprises four components and multi-scale activities including conservation planning, sustainable fish harvesting strategies, blue economy investment plans, input supply services for fisheries and aquaculture, marketing infrastructure for fish and fishery products, as well as the provision of regional conformity assessment and standardization for fish and fishery products. Training programmes will be provided to value chain actors on multiple fronts along the fish chain, especially women and youth. This will promote competitiveness in the retail and wholesale fish trade as well as facilitate cross-border corridors in the region. In addition, the project will "…support institutional capacity building for climate resilience through information service provisioning, climate buffers, and resource mobilisation towards adaptation and mitigation".[5]

The project is associated with the SADC *Regional Indicative Strategic Development Plan* (RISDP) 2020–2030, where the blue economy and fisheries agenda remain central to the vision and imperatives of regional integration.

The SADC Revised Regional Indicative Strategic Development Plan (2015–2020) and the Industrialization Strategy and Roadmap (2015–2063) both identify the blue economy as a potential areas for sustainable growth in the region. The SADC Industrialization Strategy and Roadmap (2015–2063) requires that the Blue Economy Initiative be mainstreamed in developing infrastructure required to accelerate industrialization. More recently, the African Charter on Maritime Security, Safety and Development in Africa (also known as the Lomé Charter) was adopted to address key components of the regional blue economy agenda.[6]

Back to the Future

As noted earlier, the forerunner to SADC was the Southern African Development Coordination Conference (SADCC), established in 1980. This was a fairly loose association of southern African states who were seeking ways to loosen their economic dependency on then minority-ruled South Africa (Namibia, then known as South West Africa, had yet to achieve independence from South Africa). Under the SADCC system, each country was responsible for regionally coordinating a particular industry where it had special experience or competence (for example, Zambia coordinated efforts in the mining sector). For southern Africa to better manage its blue resources, a model based on the old SADCC could prove useful.

In that regard, SADC should consider establishing a SADC Blue Economy Coordinating Unit (SADC-BECU) with a small secretariat to help harmonize member states' domestic policies for better regional cooperation. Such a secretariat would be constructed along the lines the AU suggested for a stand-alone Department of Maritime Affairs at the AU to work on, "…enhancing collaborative, concerted, cooperative, coordinated, coherent and trust building efforts throughout the continent…".[7] As the AU has not yet been able to establish a department, perhaps it is time that a REC such as SADC could take the initiative and begin the process.

The unit's first task would be to establish a Combined Exclusive Maritime Zone of Southern Africa (CEMZSA), as called for under the 2050 AIMS strategic objective number 1.[8] Such a CEMZSA could provide the legal, political and logistical framework for better coordination. It would help boost regional and international trade by reducing or eliminating administrative procedures which would make the region more competitive. Such a zone would help better ensure environmental protection, coastal and off-shore monitoring of threats including pollution, piracy, arms trafficking and harmonize the individual countries' maritime legal systems.[9]

The SADC-BECU could negotiate with the combined strength of all of its members with such important groupings and organizations as the Indian Ocean Commission, the Indian Ocean Rim Association, the South East Atlantic Fisheries Organization, the Western Indian Ocean Marine Science Association, Coastal Oceans Research and Development in the Indian Ocean (CORDIO), and the Indian Ocean Naval Symposium (IONS), Intergovernmental Oceanographic Commission, the Commission on the Limits of the Continental Shelf, Convention on Migratory Species, Commonwealth Secretariat, Global Ocean Acidification Observing Network, World Ocean Council, CBD Sustainable Oceans Initiative, UNEP Green Economy Initiative, Global Ocean Commission (GOC), Global Ocean Forum, the IOC/UNESCO Global Ocean Observing System (GOOS), World Bank (IBRD), International Maritime Organisation, International Seabed Authority, UN Regional Seas Programme, Ocean Acidification International Coordination Centre and UN specialized agencies including UNDOALOS (UNCLOS), UNDP, UNEP, UNESCO, UNFAO, UNIDO and the UNWTO.

Under SADC-BECU, a participating member state would provide the lead coordination efforts by appointing a lead ministry to work with its counterpart in the other member countries. Tasks could include better support for women and youth SMEs in eco-tourism, fish processing sales; harmonizing better fish quality control for sanitary conditions; improving conditions for increased investment and PPPs in the blue economy sectors; developing early warning systems for blue economy sectors (e.g. fishing and marine transportation); creating regional blue economy investment trust funds; encouraging fish sanctuaries and networks of regional marine protected areas; promoting maritime security; energy development; helping with technology transfer, training, joint blue bond financing and other initiatives in a number of sectors, as outlined below.

Energy, Ports, Marine Spatial Planning, Marine Pollution: South Africa

(Lead ministries: Forestry, Fisheries and the Environment; Public Service Administration; Public Works and Infrastructure.)

South Africa is the region's leader in renewable energy. For example, there are 19 wind energy developments with more than 600 wind turbines. South Africa is leading the region in producing wave energy[10] and is in an excellent position to share its expertise.

Further, South Africa has the most efficient and developed ports in the region. SADCs 2012 *Regional Infrastructure Development Master Plan*, identified six challenges to maritime transport in Southern Africa:

- Multi-modal interface management: Road transport vehicles in port areas often impede efficient operations.
- Material handling ability: Many ports are unable to handle materials correctly, regardless of their apparent capacity to do so.
- Customs and trade facilitation: Freight is often delayed for up to two months due to ineffective customs procedures that render supply chains ineffective.
- Location management: Most ports lie near densely populated industrial zones that limit necessary expansion.
- Access issues: Access roads often cross congested business, industrial, and residential areas, causing delays; railways still follow the outdated break-bulk rail system.
- Port berths: Demand for berths is approaching or exceeding capacity in most ports.[11]

Given that there are 20 ports in the SADC member countries, South Africa couple play a key role in heling coordinate port expansion and possible consolidation. Such development should include potential Public Private Partnerships and the SADC-BECU should work closely with the Port Management Association of Eastern and Southern Africa, an international organisation that promotes institutional reform of marine transport in the region.

South Africa became the first African country to adopt Marine Spatial Planning (MSP) legislation, in 2017. A national policy to fast track the oceans economy provides a challenge for ecosystem-based approaches to MSP due to lack of data and regulatory gaps. Nonetheless, South Africa could share its expertise.

Marine pollution, especially plastics, poses serious risks across the spectrum: to human health, marine nurseries, the food chain, marine ecosystems and coastal tourism. The litter consists largely of plastic waste discarded into rivers and beaches, which then enters the ocean through storm water runoff or sometimes discharged at sea from ships.

The UN Environment Programme estimates that eight million metric tonnes of plastic ends up in oceans every year. Plastic can have a lifespan of 450 years and never fully degrades, but rather shrinks into smaller pieces of plastic called microplastics.

South Africa (along with Angola and Namibia) are parties to the Abidjan Convention for Cooperation in the Protection, Management and Development of the Marine and Coastal Environment of the Atlantic Coast of the West, Central and Southern Africa region.[12]

South Africa is making efforts to address the challenge of marine pollution. For example the South African Department of Environment, Forestry and Fisheries has joined forces with local officials, non-profit groups, such as Coastwatch and Plastics SA, a privately-owned company, to reduce marine litter in five river systems in Kwazulu-Natal. The project includes increased litter collection and community-led waste sorting and recycling. This should reduce litter generation at its source, and thus lessen the amount of pollution that reaches the ocean. The project is designed to help South Africa achieve its targets under Sustainable Development Goal 14.1, where the country committed to preventing and reducing marine pollution by 2025, as well as Sustainable Development Goal 6.3 to improve water quality by 2030 through reducing pollution.[13]

Fisheries and Seafood Processing and Aquaculture: Namibia

(Lead ministry: Fisheries and Marine Resources.)

Namibia is Africa's primary exporter of fish and fish products. According to the FAO,[14] Namibia's marine capture fisheries primarily includes the industrial fisheries such as demersal trawl fishery (hake and monk species) a midwater trawl fishery (adult horse mackerel), the purse seine fishery (sardine and juvenile horse mackerel), a large pelagic fishery (tuna, swordfish and large pelagic sharks), and a rock lobster and deep-sea red crab fishery. The large pelagic sub-sector was established after Namibia's independence and concentrated on line fishery of albacore tuna. It includes a sashimi longline fleet (which freezes fish at temperatures warmer than the sashimi vessels), targeting other tunas, swordfish, large pelagic sharks and shortfin mako.

Namibia's relatively new marine aquaculture sector produces molluscan shellfish. There are nine farms along the coast with nodes at Walvis Bay-Swakopmund, Luderitz and Oranjemund. The oyster industry is expanding attracting significant investment. Namibia's cannery operations are relatively efficient and there is scope for technical training and technology transfer.

Blue Financing, Biodiversity, Marine Parks and Illegal Fishing: Seychelles

(Lead ministries: Fisheries; Agriculture, Climate Change and Environment.)

As discussed earlier, Seychelles is a world leader in Blue Bond financing for development and marine protection. There are six marine national parks in the Seychelles, administered by Seychelles National Environment Commission (SNEC), which falls under the Department of the Environment. Such parks are essential for protecting and enhancing marine biodiversity.

Seychelles was the first country from the African region to adopt the SmartFish Project, sponsored by Indian Ocean Tuna Commission (IOTC) and the European Union. The project was focused on reinforcing the country's ability to enforce the IOTC resolution based on the UN Food and Agriculture Organization's agreement to prevent illegal, unreported and unregulated (IUU) fishing. This is important to ensure that illegally harvested fish do not enter regional trade.

Artisanal Fisheries: Mozambique

(Lead ministries: The Sea, Inland Waters and Fisheries; Industry and Commerce.)

Mozambique has 1,500 miles of coastline (equal to the distance between Spain to Denmark). In coastal communities, millions of people depend on fisheries for jobs and protein. Half of Mozambicans live in the coastal zone, and its small-scale fishers catch 85% of the country's fish.

Most of the people living the coastal areas of Mozambique are artisanal fishers. This sector is an important sources of employment, income and food. However, because of low productivity and undeveloped fish processing, marketing income from artisanal fishery is low.

In addition, overfishing and destructive fishing techniques are diminishing fish catches and degrading ecosystems. Mozambique's artisanal catch has declined by as much as 30% over the last 25 years. Climate change will likely worsen this issue, as Mozambique's coasts are vulnerable to sea level rise, cyclones, and flooding.[15]

Mozambique has begun an innovative project, *Fish Forever*, that could serve as a model for other coastal communities in the SADC region. The project wants to establish managed access areas that provide fishing communities clear rights to fish in certain areas; create networks of fully-protected and community-led no-take marine reserves to replenish and sustain fish populations and protect critical habitat; build community engagement and effective management bodies to support local decision-making; enable fishers to adopt more sustainable and better-regulated fishing behaviors (e.g., become a registered fisher; record fish catch; respect fishing regulations;

participate in fisheries management); collect, disseminate and help fishing communities use data for decision-making; advance coastal fishing communities' inclusion in financial and market opportunities to increase household resilience; mobilize public and private investment in coastal fisheries and marine natural resources; and, promote and sustain a community-based management approach.[16]

Coastal Community Development: Madagascar

(Lead ministry: Communities.)

Madagascar's vast coast poses challenges for sustainable development, especially in poor, remote coastal communities. There, the lack of formal education makes it hard to disseminate knowledge among communities and encourage best practices. In an effort to combat these problems, the country is experimenting with locally managed marine areas (LMMAs).[17] These are not marine protected areas but are small parts of coastal waters that are under community management. According to *Mihari*, a network of LMMAs:

> This includes deciding which sites to fish, what to leave undisturbed, which gear to use, and what species to harvest. There is a particular emphasis on coastal residents setting the agenda, not outsiders... it is blending traditional know-how with recently acquired knowledge about marine spatial planning, animal behavior and the intricacies of oceanic ecosystems.[18]

Such a program could help other remote coastal communities in SADC.

Tourism: Mauritius

(Lead ministry: Tourism.)

Mauritius's tourism sector, as discussed earlier, is a major economic driver for its economy. Recently Mauritius has been looked at as a green tourism destination and it has made significant efforts to develop sustainable tourism activities over the past decade.[19] Environmental protection has taken on an increasingly important role, especially on its beaches as this is where its tourists want to visit.

One of the most serious problems that Mauritius faces (as do most of the other SADC coastal states) is coral reef destruction due to global warming and dynamite fishing, which destroy the reefs. Mauritius (along with Seychelles), have accessed a new US$10 million grant from the UNDP to restore their reef ecosystems.[20] The six-year project will focus on coral reef restoration which is essential for the nations' growing tourism industries which account for over 30% of national GDP and employ approximately half the population and at the same time ensuring food security for fishers. If successful, this project could be a model for other states in the region. Mauritius could also provide guidance on recreational marine fisheries related to tourism.

Off-shore Mining: Angola

(Lead ministries: Geology and Mines; Industry; Energy and Water.)

Angola is sub-Saharan Africa's second-largest oil producer and most of the oil exploration and extraction take place off shore (although the country has been conducting exploration inland in recent years). While far from perfect, it generally has taken a balanced approach to environmental, social, and governance (ESG) standards. Indeed, Angola's 2010 constitution established the country's Environmental Framework Act for protecting the environment. According to Article 12, "The State shall promote the protection and conservation of natural resources guiding the exploitation and use thereof for the benefit of the community as a whole."[21]

As most other SADC coastal members have off-shore oil and gas industries, or are engaged in exploration, Angola could provide the technology and policies needed to ensure that the sector is sustainable.

Piracy: Tanzania

(Lead ministries: Defense & National Service; East African Cooperation.)

The Indian Ocean is an important global marine navigation route, and some of the world's worst maritime piracy incidents have taken place there. In 2005, the UN's International Maritime Organization noted an increase in piracy attacks in the Gulf of Aden, at the entrance to the Indian Ocean. There had been only a few attacks in the previous decade, but then there was a sharp rise in 2005, to more than ten. That year, and in each of the subsequent two years, there were roughly a dozen attacks. From 2007 to 2008, the situation got worse: the number of attacks went to 51 in 2007 and then to 111 in 2008.[22] Pirate attacks in the region peaked in 2011, when 237 incidents were recorded, and fell to 14 between 2015 and 2020 (and none since 2017). This decline is a result of regional joint efforts to reduce crimes at sea.

Sea piracy has been an important issue for Tanzania. For example, in 2006 Tanzania received 20 luxury cruise liners full of tourists but the figure dwindled down to just two ships in 2010.[23] Cargo ships at the port of Dar es Salaam Port were affected: vessels flow in Tanzania dropped from 1,621 in 2007 to 1,228 in 2010. Further, the amount of cargo has decreased from 1.7 million metric tons in 2007 to 1.3 million in 2009. Also trade dropped from 2.0 million 20-Feet Container Equivalent Unit (TEU) in 2007 to 1.4 in 2009. Tanzania could take the lead in sharing its experience in cooperative anti-piracy efforts with other SADC members.

Artisanal Industry: Comoros

(Lead ministries: Agriculture, Fisheries & Environment; Economy, Investments & Economic Integration.)

Comoros is one of the poorest countries in the world, with about half of its population living below the poverty line. Nearly 80% of the population is employed in agriculture, primarily subsistence farming with very few natural resources.

The small industrial sector consists of a few food processing companies. Vanilla packaging plants, essential oil extraction, and furniture manufacture are generally small artisan industries. They represent less than 5% of the GDP with an annual growth of 2.3% according to the UNDP.[24]

The manufacturing industry is not well developed and involves mainly artisans and those involved in handcrafts for export, although there are other small industries geared toward the domestic market. These industries produce yogurt, plastics, shoes and handicrafts.

There are a number of factors that restrict the growth of the industrial sector: a shortage of skilled labor and raw materials, the geographically isolation, poor transportation and the high cost of electricity (energy is produced mostly by wood products and imported petroleum). However, the government is working to privatize and revitalize industrial and commercial enterprises by upgrading education and technical training and to diversify exports.

According to UNESCO, small scale artisanal production is important because of cultural diversity by linking the craft and the identity. It can help to show craft industries throughout the ages and its role to transfer traditional and cultural life for future generations.[25] Thus, by sharing its efforts to enhance small-scale, coastal artisanal industrialization, Comoros could prove to be an excellent resource for the region.

Coastal Culture Enhancement: DRC

(Lead ministry: Culture and Arts.)

With globalization, coastal culture has changed for all of the SADC members. With one of the strongest and diverse cultures in the region, DRC could offer unique examples. According to the Friends of the Congo, "Observing from ethnic groups, languages, religions, literature, theatre, sculptures, masks, music and fashion, Congo is, without a doubt, one of the most remarkable and exceptional artistic centers that Africa has to offer."[26]

Inland/Landlocked States Priorities: Rotating Basis

SADC's five inland, land-locked states (Lesotho, Malawi, Eswatini (Swaziland), Zambia and Zimbabwe) have important interests in accessing coastal and marine resources.[27] As a part of SADC-BECU, each state, on an annual basis, could be the chair and examine ways as how to better ensure long term access to ports and equitably share the bounty of the blue economy with the littoral members. Such protection of "… the right of access to sea and freedom of transit of goods for landly-connected stares" is identified as strategic objective number 11 in the *2050 AIMS.* [28]

The UNCLOS confirms landlocked states' right of access to and from the sea via the "freedom of transit through the territory of transit States by all means of transport".[29] However, such access is dependent on bilateral or multilateral agreements. The UNCLOS says that these agreements may:

> provide for free zones or other customs facilities, for the convenience of traffic in transit, at the ports of entry and exit in the transit states; not provide for traffic in transit to be subject to any customs duties, taxes or other charges except charges levied for specific services rendered in connection with such traffic; and may not subject the means of transport in transit and other facilities, provided for and used by landlocked states, to taxes or charges higher than those levied for the use of means of transport of the transit state.[30]

Currently there are several corridor agreements in the region, including the several that connect to the Namibian port of Walvis Bay: the Trans-Kalahari corridor (connecting Gaborone, Botswana with Johannesburg, South Africa), Trans-Caprivi Corridor (that connects

Lusaka, Zambia, Harare, Zimbabwe and Lubumbashi, RDC), the Trans-Cunene Corridor (connecting Lubango, Angola) and the Trans-Oranje Corridor (connecting to Cape Town, South Africa). Other such agreements should be developed.

In addition, the UNCLOS has provisions for landlocked states to exploit living resources of the coastal states' EEZs. However, as this provision is not as clear-cut as the right to access, it is important that the SADC-BECU codify such access.

In conclusion, while there are other important regional maritime issues to address, the above offers a blueprint for a start to deeper regional cooperation. Perhaps the best way forward is to do both more and less. In other words, southern Africa's blue economy should increase the overall wealth of its regional states derived from ocean and coastal resources, while at the same time adjusting resource use to biologically sustainable levels. To succeed, each country must chart a course that is appropriate to its development ambitions, but it is essential that efforts be completed in a regionally coordinated manner. Should the region decide to take the path that is suggested here, it will take determined efforts at all levels of society. Such efforts will be richly rewarded in a region whose blue economy can lay the foundation for sustainable growth.

Notes

1 The Tripartite regional economic communities include the Common Market for Eastern and Southern Africa (COMESA), the East African Community (ECA) and the Southern Africa Development Community (SADC).
2 Attri & Bohler-Muller (2018).
3 See Draper (2010) and Fioramonti and Mattheis (2015).
4 CIA (2017).
5 https://www.sadc.int/news-events/news/sadc-afdb-and-partners-launch-pro fishblue-programme-sadc-region/.
6 African Union Commission (2016).
7 African Union (2012).
8 African Union (2012).
9 There are a number of other ambitious initiatives to consider such as an SADC-owned shipping line.
10 Belletti & McBride (2021).
11 https://www.sadc.int/files/7513/5293/3530/Regional_Infrastructure_Develo pment_Master_Plan_Executive_Summary.pdf.
12 https://www.sardc.net/en/southern-african-news-features/managing-marine -litter-in-southern-africa/.
13 https://www.unep.org/news-and-stories/story/south-africa-aims-stop-marin e-litter-its-source.

14 United Nations Food and Agriculture Organization (2022).
15 https://rare.org/program/fish-forever-in-mozambique/.
16 http://rare.org. program/Fish Forever in Mozambique – Rare.
17 https://news.mongabay.com/2022/03/small-scale-fishers-have-a-ph-d-in-the-ocean-qa-with-vatosoa-rakotondrazafy/.
18 https://mihari-network.org/en/news/biggest-ever-meeting-of-madagascar-fishers/.
19 https://www.mymauritius.travel/experiences/sustainable-tourism.
20 https://www.preventionweb.net/news/protect-billion-dollar-tourism-industry-mauritius-and-seychelles-restore-their-coral-reefs-new.
21 https://jpt.spe.org/column-angolas-oil-and-gas-industry-can-thrive-alongside-its-rich-biodiversity.
22 https://lithub.com/on-the-ebb-and-flow-of-21st-century-maritime-piracy/.
23 https://safety4sea.com/tanzanian-nation-keen-to-curb-piracy/.
24 https://www.google.com/search?q=artisanal+industries+comoros&client=firefox-b-1-d&sxsrf=ALiCzsbiEUUnm1gOENxQ3NaWJUmUnDXdCA:1655492637412&ei=HdCsYoTeGN6ekPIPleuF6Ao&start=10&sa=N&ved=2ahUKEwjE4NLUlrX4AhVeD0QIHZV1Aa0Q8NMDegQIARBN&biw=1920&bih=955&dpr=1.
25 https://en.unesco.org/creativity/policy-monitoring-platform/awareness-forum-craft-industries.
26 https://friendsofthecongo.org/congolese-culture/.
27 In its *2050 AIMS*, the AU uses the term "landly-connected" as opposed to land locked.
28 African Union (2012).
29 Swanepoel (2020).
30 UN Convention on the Law of the Sea (December 10, 1982), art. 124(1)(a), https://www.un.org/depts/los/convention_agreements/ convention_overview_convention.htm.

Appendix A – United Nations Convention on the Law of the Sea (relevant sections)

Section 1. General Provisions

Article 2

1   The sovereignty of a coastal State extends, beyond its land territory and internal waters and, in the case of an archipelagic State, its archipelagic waters, to an adjacent belt of sea, described as the territorial sea.
2   This sovereignty extends to the air space over the territorial sea as well as to its bed and subsoil.
3   The sovereignty over the territorial sea is exercised subject to this Convention and to other rules of international law.

Section 2. Limits of the Territorial Sea

Every State has the right to establish the breadth of its territorial sea up to a limit not exceeding 12 nautical miles, measured from baselines determined in accordance with this Convention.

Article 4

The outer limit of the territorial sea is the line every point of which is at a distance from the nearest point of the baseline equal to the breadth of the territorial sea.

Article 5

Except where otherwise provided in this Convention, the normal baseline for measuring the breadth of the territorial sea is the low-water line along the coast as marked on large-scale charts officially recognized by the coastal State.

Article 6

In the case of islands situated on atolls or of islands having fringing reefs, the baseline for measuring the breadth of the territorial sea is the seaward low-water line of the reef, as shown by the appropriate symbol on charts officially recognized by the coastal State.

Article 7

Straight Baselines

1   In localities where the coastline is deeply indented and cut into, or if there is a fringe of islands along the coast in its immediate vicinity, the method of straight baselines joining appropriate points may be employed in drawing the baseline from which the breadth of the territorial sea is measured.
2   Where because of the presence of a delta and other natural conditions the coastline is highly unstable, the appropriate points may be selected along the furthest seaward extent of the low-water line and, notwithstanding subsequent regression of the low-water line, the straight baselines shall remain effective until changed by the coastal State in accordance with this Convention.
3   The drawing of straight baselines must not depart to any appreciable extent from the general direction of the coast, and the sea areas lying within the lines must be sufficiently closely linked to the land domain to be subject to the regime of internal waters.
4   Straight baselines shall not be drawn to and from low-tide elevations, unless lighthouses or similar installations which are permanently above sea level have been built on them or except in instances where the drawing of baselines to and from such elevations has received general international recognition.
5   Where the method of straight baselines is applicable under paragraph 1, account may be taken, in determining particular baselines, of economic interests peculiar to the region concerned, the reality and the importance of which are clearly evidenced by long usage.
6   The system of straight baselines may not be applied by a State in such a manner as to cut off the territorial sea of another State from the high seas or an exclusive economic zone.

Article 8

Internal waters

1   Except as provided in Part IV, waters on the landward side of the baseline of the territorial sea form part of the internal waters of the State.
2   Where the establishment of a straight baseline in accordance with the method set forth in article 7 has the effect of enclosing as internal waters areas which had not previously been considered as such, a right of innocent passage as provided in this Convention shall exist in those waters.

Article 9

If a river flows directly into the sea, the baseline shall be a straight line across the mouth of the river between points on the low-water line of its banks.

Article 10

1   This article relates only to bays the coasts of which belong to a single State.
2   For the purposes of this Convention, a bay is a well-marked indentation whose penetration is in such proportion to the width of its mouth as to contain land-locked waters and constitute more than a mere curvature of the coast. An indentation shall not, however, be regarded as a bay unless its area is as large as, or larger than, that of the semi-circle whose diameter is a line drawn across the mouth of that indentation.
3   For the purpose of measurement, the area of an indentation is that lying between the low-water mark around the shore of the indentation and a line joining the low-water mark of its natural entrance points. Where, because of the presence of islands, an indentation has more than one mouth, the semi-circle shall be drawn on a line as long as the sum total of the lengths of the lines across the different mouths. Islands within an indentation shall be included as if they were part of the water area of the indentation.
4   If the distance between the low-water marks of the natural entrance points of a bay does not exceed 24 nautical miles, a closing line may be drawn between these two low-water marks, and the waters enclosed thereby shall be considered as internal waters.

5   Where the distance between the low-water marks of the natural entrance points of a bay exceeds 24 nautical miles, a straight baseline of 24 nautical miles shall be drawn within the bay in such a manner as to enclose the maximum area of water that is possible with a line of that length.

6   The foregoing provisions do not apply to so-called "historic" bays, or in any case where the system of straight baselines provided for in article 7 is applied.

Article 11

For the purpose of delimiting the territorial sea, the outermost permanent harbour works which form an integral part of the harbour system are regarded as forming part of the coast. Off-shore installations and artificial islands shall not be considered as permanent harbour works.

Article 12

Roadsteads which are normally used for the loading, unloading and anchoring of ships, and which would otherwise be situated wholly or partly outside the outer limit of the territorial sea, are included in the territorial sea.

Article 13

1   A low-tide elevation is a naturally formed area of land which is surrounded by and above water at low tide but submerged at high tide. Where a low-tide elevation is situated wholly or partly at a distance not exceeding the breadth of the territorial sea from the mainland or an island, the low-water line on that elevation may be used as the baseline for measuring the breadth of the territorial sea.

2   Where a low-tide elevation is wholly situated at a distance exceeding the breadth of the territorial sea from the mainland or an island, it has no territorial sea of its own.

Article 14

The coastal State may determine baselines in turn by any of the methods provided for in the foregoing articles to suit different conditions.

Article 15

Where the coasts of two States are opposite or adjacent to each other, neither of the two States is entitled, failing agreement between them to the contrary, to extend its territorial sea beyond the median line every point of which is equidistant from the nearest points on the baselines from which the breadth of the territorial seas of each of the two States is measured. The above provision does not apply, however, where it is necessary by reason of historic title or other special circumstances to delimit the territorial seas of the two States in a way which is at variance therewith.

Article 16

1   The baselines for measuring the breadth of the territorial sea determined in accordance with articles 7, 9 and 10, or the limits derived therefrom, and the lines of delimitation drawn in accordance with articles 12 and 15 shall be shown on charts of a scale or scales adequate for ascertaining their position. Alternatively, a list of geographical coordinates of points, specifying the geodetic datum, may be substituted.

2   The coastal State shall give due publicity to such charts or lists of geographical coordinates and shall deposit a copy of each such chart or list with the Secretary-General of the United Nations.

Section 3. Innocent Passage in the Territorial Sea, Subsection A. Rules Applicable To All Ships

Article 17

Subject to this Convention, ships of all States, whether coastal or land-locked, enjoy the right of innocent passage through the territorial sea.

Article 18

1   Passage means navigation through the territorial sea for the purpose of:

   a   traversing that sea without entering internal waters or calling at a roadstead or port facility outside internal waters; or b   proceeding to or from internal waters or a call at such roadstead or port facility.

2   Passage shall be continuous and expeditious. However, passage includes stopping and anchoring, but only in so far as the same are incidental to ordinary navigation or are rendered necessary by *force majeure* or distress or for the purpose of rendering assistance to persons, ships or aircraft in danger or distress.

Article 19

1   Passage is innocent so long as it is not prejudicial to the peace, good order or security of the coastal State. Such passage shall take place in conformity with this Convention and with other rules of international law.

2   Passage of a foreign ship shall be considered to be prejudicial to the peace, good order or security of the coastal State if in the territorial sea it engages in any of the following activities:

a   any threat or use of force against the sovereignty, territorial integrity or political independence of the coastal State, or in any other manner in violation of the principles of international law embodied in the Charter of the United Nations;

b   any exercise or practice with weapons of any kind;

c   any act aimed at collecting information to the prejudice of the defence or security of the coastal State;

d   any act of propaganda aimed at affecting the defence or security of the coastal State;

e   the launching, landing or taking on board of any aircraft;

f   the launching, landing or taking on board of any military device;

g   the loading or unloading of any commodity, currency or person contrary to the customs, fiscal, immigration or sanitary laws and regulations of the coastal State;

h   any act of wilful and serious pollution contrary to this Convention;

i   any fishing activities;

j   the carrying out of research or survey activities;

k   any act aimed at interfering with any systems of communication or any other facilities or installations of the coastal State;

l   any other activity not having a direct bearing on passage.

Article 20

In the territorial sea, submarines and other underwater vehicles are required to navigate on the surface and to show their flag.

Article 21

1   The coastal State may adopt laws and regulations, in conformity with the provisions of this Convention and other rules of international law, relating to innocent passage through the territorial sea, in respect of all or any of the following:

    a   the safety of navigation and the regulation of maritime traffic;
    b   the protection of navigational aids and facilities and other facilities or installations;
    c   the protection of cables and pipelines;
    d   the conservation of the living resources of the sea;
    e   the prevention of infringement of the fisheries laws and regulations of the coastal State;
    f   the preservation of the environment of the coastal State and the prevention, reduction and control of pollution thereof;
    g   marine scientific research and hydrographic surveys;
    h   the prevention of infringement of the customs, fiscal, immigration or sanitary laws and regulations of the coastal State.

2   Such laws and regulations shall not apply to the design, construction, manning or equipment of foreign ships unless they are giving effect to generally accepted international rules or standards.
3   The coastal State shall give due publicity to all such laws and regulations.
4   Foreign ships exercising the right of innocent passage through the territorial sea shall comply with all such laws and regulations and all generally accepted international regulations relating to the prevention of collisions at sea.

Article 22

1   The coastal State may, where necessary having regard to the safety of navigation, require foreign ships exercising the right of innocent passage through its territorial sea to use such sea lanes and traffic separation schemes as it may designate or prescribe for the regulation of the passage of ships.

2   In particular, tankers, nuclear-powered ships and ships carrying nuclear or other inherently dangerous or noxious substances or materials may be required to confine their passage to such sea lanes.

3   In the designation of sea lanes and the prescription of traffic separation schemes under this article, the coastal State shall take into account:

   a   the recommendations of the competent international organization;
   b   any channels customarily used for international navigation;
   c   the special characteristics of particular ships and channels; and
   d   the density of traffic.

4   The coastal State shall clearly indicate such sea lanes and traffic separation schemes on charts to which due publicity shall be given.

Article 23

Foreign nuclear-powered ships and ships carrying nuclear or other inherently dangerous or noxious substances shall, when exercising the right of innocent passage through the territorial sea, carry documents and observe special precautionary measures established for such ships by international agreements.

Article 24

1   The coastal State shall not hamper the innocent passage of foreign ships through the territorial sea except in accordance with this Convention. In particular, in the application of this Convention or of any laws or regulations adopted in conformity with this onvention, the coastal State shall not:

   a   impose requirements on foreign ships which have the practical effect of denying or impairing the right of innocent passage; or
   b   discriminate in form or in fact against the ships of any State or against ships carrying cargoes to, from or on behalf of any State.

2   The coastal State shall give appropriate publicity to any danger to navigation, of which it has knowledge, within its territorial sea.

Article 25

1   The coastal State may take the necessary steps in its territorial sea to prevent passage which is not innocent.
2   In the case of ships proceeding to internal waters or a call at a port facility outside internal waters, the coastal State also has the right to take the necessary steps to prevent any breach of the conditions to which admission of those ships to internal waters or such a call is subject.
3   The coastal State may, without discrimination in form or in fact among foreign ships, suspend temporarily in specified areas of its territorial sea the innocent passage of foreign ships if such suspension is essential for the protection of its security, including weapons exercises. Such suspension shall take effect only after having been duly published.

Article 26

1   No charge may be levied upon foreign ships by reason only of their passage through the territorial sea.
2   Charges may be levied upon a foreign ship passing through the territorial sea as payment only for specific services rendered to the ship. These charges shall be levied without discrimination.

Section 4. Contiguous Zone

Article 33

1   In a zone contiguous to its territorial sea, described as the contiguous zone, the coastal State may exercise the control necessary to:

   a   prevent infringement of its customs, fiscal, immigration or sanitary laws and regulations within its territory or territorial sea;
   b   punish infringement of the above laws and regulations committed within its territory or territorial sea.

2 The contiguous zone may not extend beyond 24 nautical miles from the baselines from which the breadth of the territorial sea is measured.

Part V Exclusive Economic Zone

Article 55

The exclusive economic zone is an area beyond and adjacent to the territorial sea, subject to the specific legal regime established in this Part, under which the rights and jurisdiction of the coastal State and the rights and freedoms of other States are governed by the relevant provisions of this Convention.

Article 56

1 In the exclusive economic zone, the coastal State has:

   a sovereign rights for the purpose of exploring and exploiting, conserving and managing the natural resources, whether living or non-living, of the waters superjacent to the seabed and of the seabed and its subsoil, and with regard to other activities for the economic exploitation and exploration of the zone, such as the production of energy from the water, currents and winds;

   b jurisdiction as provided for in the relevant provisions of this Convention with regard to:

      i the establishment and use of artificial islands, installations and structures;

      ii marine scientific research;

      iii the protection and preservation of the marine environment;

   c other rights and duties provided for in this Convention.

2 In exercising its rights and performing its duties under this Convention in the exclusive economic zone, the coastal State shall have due regard to the rights and duties of other States and shall act in a manner compatible with the provisions of this Convention.

3 The rights set out in this article with respect to the seabed and subsoil shall be exercised in accordance with Part VI.

Article 57

The exclusive economic zone shall not extend beyond 200 nautical miles from the baselines from which the breadth of the territorial sea is measured.

Article 58

1   In the exclusive economic zone, all States, whether coastal or land-locked, enjoy, subject to the relevant provisions of this Convention, the freedoms referred to in article 87 of navigation and overflight and of the laying of submarine cables and pipelines, and other internationally lawful uses of the sea related to these freedoms, such as those associated with the operation of ships, aircraft and submarine cables and pipelines, and compatible with the other provisions of this Convention.

2   Articles 88 to 115 and other pertinent rules of international law apply to the exclusive economic zone in so far as they are not incompatible with this Part.

3   In exercising their rights and performing their duties under this Convention in the exclusive economic zone, States shall have due regard to the rights and duties of the coastal State and shall comply with the laws and regulations adopted by the coastal State in accordance with the provisions of this Convention and other rules of international law in so far as they are not incompatible with this Part.

Article 59

In cases where this Convention does not attribute rights or jurisdiction to the coastal State or to other States within the exclusive economic zone, and a conflict arises between the interests of the coastal State and any other State or States, the conflict should be resolved on the basis of equity and in the light of all the relevant circumstances, taking into account the respective importance of the interests involved to the parties as well as to the international community as a whole.

Article 60

1   In the exclusive economic zone, the coastal State shall have the exclusive right to construct and to authorize and regulate the construction, operation and use of:

   a   artificial islands;

b installations and structures for the purposes provided for in
article 56 and other economic purposes;

c installations and structures which may interfere with the
exercise of the rights of the coastal State in the zone.

2 The coastal State shall have exclusive jurisdiction over such artificial
islands, installations and structures, including jurisdiction
with regard to customs, fiscal, health, safety and immigration laws
and regulations.

3 Due notice must be given of the construction of such artificial
islands, installations or structures, and permanent means for
giving warning of their presence must be maintained. Any installations
or structures which are abandoned or disused shall be
removed to ensure safety of navigation, taking into account any
generally accepted international standards established in this
regard by the competent international organization. Such removal
shall also have due regard to fishing, the protection of the marine
environment and the rights and duties of other States. Appropriate
publicity shall be given to the depth, position and
dimensions of any installations or structures not entirely removed.

4 The coastal State may, where necessary, establish reasonable safety
zones around such artificial islands, installations and structures in
which it may take appropriate measures to ensure the safety both
of navigation and of the artificial islands, installations and
structures.

5 The breadth of the safety zones shall be determined by the coastal
State, taking into account applicable international standards. Such
zones shall be designed to ensure that they are reasonably related
to the nature and function of the artificial islands, installations or
structures, and shall not exceed a distance of 500 metres around
them, measured from each point of their outer edge, except as
authorized by generally accepted international standards or as
recommended by the competent international organization. Due
notice shall be given of the extent of safety zones.

6 All ships must respect these safety zones and shall comply with
generally accepted international standards regarding navigation in
the vicinity of artificial islands, installations, structures and safety
zones.

7 Artificial islands, installations and structures and the safety zones
around them may not be established where interference may be

caused to the use of recognized sea lanes essential to international navigation.

8   Artificial islands, installations and structures do not possess the status of islands. They have no territorial sea of their own, and their presence does not affect the delimitation of the territorial sea, the exclusive economic zone or the continental shelf.

Article 61

1   The coastal State shall determine the allowable catch of the living resources in its exclusive economic zone.

2   The coastal State, taking into account the best scientific evidence available to it, shall ensure through proper conservation and management measures that the maintenance of the living resources in the exclusive economic zone is not endangered by over-exploitation. As appropriate, the coastal State and competent international organizations, whether subregional, regional or global, shall cooperate to this end.

3   Such measures shall also be designed to maintain or restore populations of harvested species at levels which can produce the maximum sustainable yield, as qualified by relevant environmental and economic factors, including the economic needs of coastal fishing communities and the special requirements of developing States, and taking into account fishing patterns, the inter-dependence of stocks and any generally recommended international minimum standards, whether subregional, regional or global.

4   In taking such measures the coastal State shall take into consideration the effects on species associated with or dependent upon harvested species with a view to maintaining or restoring populations of such associated or dependent species above levels at which their reproduction may become seriously threatened.

5   Available scientific information, catch and fishing effort statistics, and other data relevant to the conservation of fish stocks shall be contributed and exchanged on a regular basis through competent international organizations, whether subregional, regional or global, where appropriate and with participation by all States concerned, including States whose nationals are allowed to fish in the exclusive economic zone.

Article 62

1   The coastal State shall promote the objective of optimum utiliza-
    tion of the living resources in the exclusive economic zone without
    prejudice to article 61.
2   The coastal State shall determine its capacity to harvest the living
    resources of the exclusive economic zone. Where the coastal State
    does not have the capacity to harvest the entire allowable catch, it
    shall, through agreements or other arrangements and pursuant to
    the terms, conditions, laws and regulations referred to in para-
    graph 4, give other States access to the surplus of the allowable
    catch, having particular regard to the provisions of articles 69 and
    70, especially in relation to the developing States mentioned
    therein.
3   In giving access to other States to its exclusive economic zone
    under this article, the coastal State shall take into account all
    relevant factors, including, *inter alia*, the significance of the living
    resources of the area to the economy of the coastal State con-
    cerned and its other national interests, the provisions of articles 69
    and 70, the requirements of developing States in the subregion or
    region in harvesting part of the surplus and the need to minimize
    economic dislocation in States whose nationals have habitually
    fished in the zone or which have made substantial efforts in
    research and identification of stocks.
4   Nationals of other States fishing in the exclusive economic zone
    shall comply with the conservation measures and with the other
    terms and conditions established in the laws and regulations of
    the coastal State. These laws and regulations shall be consistent
    with this Convention and may relate, *inter alia*, to the following:

    a   licensing of fishermen, fishing vessels and equipment, includ-
        ing payment of fees and other forms of remuneration, which,
        in the case of developing coastal States, may consist of ade-
        quate compensation in the field of financing, equipment and
        technology relating to the fishing industry;
    b   determining the species which may be caught, and fixing
        quotas of catch, whether in relation to particular stocks or
        groups of stocks or catch per vessel over a period of time or
        to the catch by nationals of any State during a specified
        period;
    c   regulating seasons and areas of fishing, the types, sizes and
        amount of gear, and the types, sizes and number of fishing
        vessels that may be used;

d   fixing the age and size of fish and other species that may be caught;

e   specifying information required of fishing vessels, including catch and effort statistics and vessel position reports;

f   requiring, under the authorization and control of the coastal State, the conduct of specified fisheries research programmes and regulating the conduct of such research, including the sampling of catches, disposition of samples and reporting of associated scientific data;

g   the placing of observers or trainees on board such vessels by the coastal State;

h   the landing of all or any part of the catch by such vessels in the ports of the coastal State;

i   terms and conditions relating to joint ventures or other cooperative arrangements;

j   requirements for the training of personnel and the transfer of fisheries technology, including enhancement of the coastal State's capability of undertaking fisheries research;

k   enforcement procedures.

5   Coastal States shall give due notice of conservation and management laws and regulations.

Article 63

1   Where the same stock or stocks of associated species occur within the exclusive economic zones of two or more coastal States, these States shall seek, either directly or through appropriate subregional or regional organizations, to agree upon the measures necessary to coordinate and ensure the conservation and development of such stocks without prejudice to the other provisions of this Part.

2   Where the same stock or stocks of associated species occur both within the exclusive economic zone and in an area beyond and adjacent to the zone, the coastal State and the States fishing for such stocks in the adjacent area shall seek, either directly or through appropriate subregional or regional organizations, to agree upon the measures necessary for the conservation of these stocks in the adjacent area.

Article 64

1 The coastal State and other States whose nationals fish in the region for the highly migratory species listed in Annex I shall cooperate directly or through appropriate international organizations with a view to ensuring conservation and promoting the objective of optimum utilization of such species throughout the region, both within and beyond the exclusive economic zone. In regions for which no appropriate international organization exists, the coastal State and other States whose nationals harvest these species in the region shall cooperate to establish such an organization and participate in its work.

2 The provisions of paragraph 1 apply in addition to the other provisions of this Part.

3 Nothing in this Part restricts the right of a coastal State or the competence of an international organization, as appropriate, to prohibit, limit or regulate the exploitation of marine mammals more strictly than provided for in this Part. States shall cooperate with a view to the conservation of marine mammals and in the case of cetaceans shall in particular work through the appropriate international organizations for their conservation, management and study.

Article 66

1 States in whose rivers anadromous stocks originate shall have the primary interest in and responsibility for such stocks.

2 The State of origin of anadromous stocks shall ensure their conservation by the establishment of appropriate regulatory measures for fishing in all waters landward of the outer limits of its exclusive economic zone and for fishing provided for in paragraph 3(b). The State of origin may, after consultations with the other States referred to in paragraphs 3 and 4 fishing these stocks, establish total allowable catches for stocks originating in its rivers.

3

    a Fisheries for anadromous stocks shall be conducted only in waters landward of the outer limits of exclusive economic zones, except in cases where this provision would result in economic dislocation for a State other than the State of origin. With respect to such fishing beyond the outer limits of the exclusive economic zone, States concerned shall maintain consultations with a view to achieving agreement on terms and conditions of such fishing giving due regard to the conservation requirements and the needs of the State of origin in respect of these stocks.

b   The State of origin shall cooperate in minimizing economic dislocation in such other States fishing these stocks, taking into account the normal catch and the mode of operations of such States, and all the areas in which such fishing has occurred.

c   States referred to in subparagraph (b), participating by agreement with the State of origin in measures to renew anadromous stocks, particularly by expenditures for that purpose, shall be given special consideration by the State of origin in the harvesting of stocks originating in its rivers.

d   Enforcement of regulations regarding anadromous stocks beyond the exclusive economic zone shall be by agreement between the State of origin and the other States concerned.

4   In cases where anadromous stocks migrate into or through the waters landward of the outer limits of the exclusive economic zone of a State other than the State of origin, such State shall cooperate with the State of origin with regard to the conservation and management of such stocks.

5   The State of origin of anadromous stocks and other States fishing these stocks shall make arrangements for the implementation of the provisions of this article, where appropriate, through regional organizations.

Article 67

1   A coastal State in whose waters catadromous species spend the greater part of their life cycle shall have responsibility for the management of these species and shall ensure the ingress and egress of migrating fish.

2   Harvesting of catadromous species shall be conducted only in waters landward of the outer limits of exclusive economic zones. When conducted in exclusive economic zones, harvesting shall be subject to this article and the other provisions of this Convention concerning fishing in these zones.

3   In cases where catadromous fish migrate through the exclusive economic zone of another State, whether as juvenile or maturing fish, the management, including harvesting, of such fish shall be regulated by agreement between the State mentioned in

paragraph 1 and the other State concerned. Such agreement shall ensure the rational management of the species and take into account the responsibilities of the State mentioned in paragraph 1 for the maintenance of these species.

Article 68

This Part does not apply to sedentary species as defined in article 77, paragraph 4.

Article 69

1   Land-locked States shall have the right to participate, on an equitable basis, in the exploitation of an appropriate part of the surplus of the living resources of the exclusive economic zones of coastal States of the same subregion or region, taking into account the relevant economic and geographical circumstances of all the States concerned and in conformity with the provisions of this article and of articles 61 and 62.

2   The terms and modalities of such participation shall be established by the States concerned through bilateral, subregional or regional agreements taking into account, *inter alia*:

   a   the need to avoid effects detrimental to fishing communities or fishing industries of the coastal State;

   b   the extent to which the land-locked State, in accordance with the provisions of this article, is participating or is entitled to participate under existing bilateral, subregional or regional agreements in the exploitation of living resources of the exclusive economic zones of other coastal States;

   c   the extent to which other land-locked States and geographically disadvantaged States are participating in the exploitation of the living resources of the exclusive economic zone of the coastal State and the consequent need to avoid a particular burden for any single coastal State or a part of it;

   d   the nutritional needs of the populations of the respective States.

3   When the harvesting capacity of a coastal State approaches a point which would enable it to harvest the entire allowable catch of the living resources in its exclusive economic zone, the coastal State and other States concerned shall cooperate in the

establishment of equitable arrangements on a bilateral, sub-regional or regional basis to allow for participation of developing land-locked States of the same subregion or region in the exploitation of the living resources of the exclusive economic zones of coastal States of the subregion or region, as may be appropriate in the circumstances and on terms satisfactory to all parties. In the implementation of this provision the factors mentioned in paragraph 2 shall also be taken into account.

4   Developed land-locked States shall, under the provisions of this article, be entitled to participate in the exploitation of living resources only in the exclusive economic zones of developed coastal States of the same subregion or region having regard to the extent to which the coastal State, in giving access to other States to the living resources of its exclusive economic zone, has taken into account the need to minimize detrimental effects on fishing communities and economic dislocation in States whose nationals have habitually fished in the zone.

5   The above provisions are without prejudice to arrangements agreed upon in subregions or regions where the coastal States may grant to land-locked States of the same subregion or region equal or preferential rights for the exploitation of the living resources in the exclusive economic zones.

Article 70

1   Geographically disadvantaged States shall have the right to participate, on an equitable basis, in the exploitation of an appropriate part of the surplus of the living resources of the exclusive economic zones of coastal States of the same subregion or region, taking into account the relevant economic and geographical circumstances of all the States concerned and in conformity with the provisions of this article and of articles 61 and 62.

2   For the purposes of this Part, "geographically disadvantaged States" means coastal States, including States bordering enclosed or semi-enclosed seas, whose geographical situation makes them dependent upon the exploitation of the living resources of the exclusive economic zones of other States in the subregion or region for adequate supplies of fish for the nutritional purposes of their populations or parts thereof, and coastal States which can claim no exclusive economic zones of their own.

3   The terms and modalities of such participation shall be established by the States concerned through bilateral, subregional or regional agreements taking into account, *inter alia*:

a   the need to avoid effects detrimental to fishing communities or fishing industries of the coastal State;

b   the extent to which the geographically disadvantaged State, in accordance with the provisions of this article, is participating or is entitled to participate under existing bilateral, subregional or regional agreements in the exploitation of living resources of the exclusive economic zones of other coastal States;

c   the extent to which other geographically disadvantaged States and land-locked States are participating in the exploitation of the living resources of the exclusive economic zone of the coastal State and the consequent need to avoid a particular burden for any single coastal State or a part of it;

d   the nutritional needs of the populations of the respective States.

4   When the harvesting capacity of a coastal State approaches a point which would enable it to harvest the entire allowable catch of the living resources in its exclusive economic zone, the coastal State and other States concerned shall cooperate in the establishment of equitable arrangements on a bilateral, subregional or regional basis to allow for participation of developing geographically disadvantaged States of the same subregion or region in the exploitation of the living resources of the exclusive economic zones of coastal States of the subregion or region, as may be appropriate in the circumstances and on terms satisfactory to all parties. In the implementation of this provision the factors mentioned in paragraph 3 shall also be taken into account.

5   Developed geographically disadvantaged States shall, under the provisions of this article, be entitled to participate in the exploitation of living resources only in the exclusive economic zones of developed coastal States of the same subregion or region having regard to the extent to which the coastal State, in giving access to other States to the living resources of its exclusive economic zone, has taken into account the need to minimize detrimental effects on fishing communities and economic dislocation in States whose nationals have habitually fished in the zone.

6   The above provisions are without prejudice to arrangements
agreed upon in subregions or regions where the coastal States may
grant to geographically disadvantaged States of the same subregion or region equal or preferential rights for the exploitation of
the living resources in the exclusive economic zones.

Article 71

The provisions of articles 69 and 70 do not apply in the case of a
coastal State whose economy is overwhelmingly dependent on the
exploitation of the living resources of its exclusive economic zone.

Article 72

1   Rights provided under articles 69 and 70 to exploit living resources shall not be directly or indirectly transferred to third States or
their nationals by lease or licence, by establishing joint ventures or
in any other manner which has the effect of such transfer unless
otherwise agreed by the States concerned.

2   The foregoing provision does not preclude the States concerned
from obtaining technical or financial assistance from third States
or international organizations in order to facilitate the exercise of
the rights pursuant to articles 69 and 70, provided that it does not
have the effect referred to in paragraph 1.

Article 73

1   The coastal State may, in the exercise of its sovereign rights to
explore, exploit, conserve and manage the living resources in the
exclusive economic zone, take such measures, including boarding,
inspection, arrest and judicial proceedings, as may be necessary to
ensure compliance with the laws and regulations adopted by it in
conformity with this Convention.

2   Arrested vessels and their crews shall be promptly released upon
the posting of reasonable bond or other security.

3   Coastal State penalties for violations of fisheries laws and regulations in the exclusive economic zone may not include imprison-
ment, in the absence of agreements to the contrary by the States
concerned, or any other form of corporal punishment.

4   In cases of arrest or detention of foreign vessels the coastal State
shall promptly notify the flag State, through appropriate channels,
of the action taken and of any penalties subsequently imposed.

Article 74

1   The delimitation of the exclusive economic zone between States with opposite or adjacent coasts shall be effected by agreement on the basis of international law, as referred to in Article 38 of the Statute of the International Court of Justice, in order to achieve an equitable solution.

2   If no agreement can be reached within a reasonable period of time, the States concerned shall resort to the procedures provided for in Part XV.

3   Pending agreement as provided for in paragraph 1, the States concerned, in a spirit of understanding and cooperation, shall make every effort to enter into provisional arrangements of a practical nature and, during this transitional period, not to jeopardize or hamper the reaching of the final agreement. Such arrangements shall be without prejudice to the final delimitation.

4   Where there is an agreement in force between the States concerned, questions relating to the delimitation of the exclusive economic zone shall be determined in accordance with the provisions of that agreement.

Article 75

1   Subject to this Part, the outer limit lines of the exclusive economic zone and the lines of delimitation drawn in accordance with article 74 shall be shown on charts of a scale or scales adequate for ascertaining their position. Where appropriate, lists of geographical coordinates of points, specifying the geodetic datum, may be substituted for such outer limit lines or lines of delimitation.

2   The coastal State shall give due publicity to such charts or lists of geographical coordinates and shall deposit a copy of each such chart or list with the Secretary-General of the United Nations.

Art X Right of Access of Land-Locked States to and from the Sea And Freedom of Transit

Article 124

1   For the purposes of this Convention:

    a   "land-locked State" means a State which has no sea-coast;

b   "transit State" means a State, with or without a sea-coast, situated between a land-locked State and the sea, through whose territory traffic in transit passes;

c   "traffic in transit" means transit of persons, baggage, goods and means of transport across the territory of one or more transit States, when the passage across such territory, with or without trans-shipment, warehousing, breaking bulk or change in the mode of transport, is only a portion of a complete journey which begins or terminates within the territory of the land-locked State;

d   "means of transport" means:

i   railway rolling stock, sea, lake and river craft and road vehicles;

ii   where local conditions so require, porters and pack animals.

2   Land-locked States and transit States may, by agreement between them, include as means of transport pipelines and gas lines and means of transport other than those included in paragraph 1.

Article 125

1   Land-locked States shall have the right of access to and from the sea for the purpose of exercising the rights provided for in this Convention including those relating to the freedom of the high seas and the common heritage of mankind. To this end, land-locked States shall enjoy freedom of transit through the territory of transit States by all means of transport.

2   The terms and modalities for exercising freedom of transit shall be agreed between the land-locked States and transit States concerned through bilateral, subregional or regional agreements.

3   Transit States, in the exercise of their full sovereignty over their territory, shall have the right to take all measures necessary to ensure that the rights and facilities provided for in this Part for land-locked States shall in no way infringe their legitimate interests.

Article 126

The provisions of this Convention, as well as special agreements relating to the exercise of the right of access to and from the sea, establishing rights and facilities on account of the special geographical position of land-locked States, are excluded from the application of the most-favoured-nation clause.

Article 127

1 Traffic in transit shall not be subject to any customs duties, taxes or other charges except charges levied for specific services rendered in connection with such traffic.
2 Means of transport in transit and other facilities provided for and used by land-locked States shall not be subject to taxes or charges higher than those levied for the use of means of transport of the transit State.

Article 128

For the convenience of traffic in transit, free zones or other customs facilities may be provided at the ports of entry and exit in the transit States, by agreement between those States and the land-locked States.

Article 129

Where there are no means of transport in transit States to give effect to the freedom of transit or where the existing means, including the port installations and equipment, are inadequate in any respect, the transit States and land-locked States concerned may cooperate in constructing or improving them.

Article 130

1 Transit States shall take all appropriate measures to avoid delays or other difficulties of a technical nature in traffic in transit.
2 Should such delays or difficulties occur, the competent authorities of the transit States and land-locked States concerned shall cooperate towards their expeditious elimination.

Article 131

Ships flying the flag of land-locked States shall enjoy treatment equal to that accorded to other foreign ships in maritime ports.

72 *Appendix*

Article 132

This Convention does not entail in any way the withdrawal of transit facilities which are greater than those provided for in this Convention and which are agreed between States Parties to this Convention or granted by a State Party. This Convention also does not preclude such grant of greater facilities in the future.

Section 2. Principles Governing the Area

Article 136

The Area and its resources are the common heritage of mankind.

Article 137

1 No State shall claim or exercise sovereignty or sovereign rights over any part of the Area or its resources, nor shall any State or natural or juridical person appropriate any part thereof. No such claim or exercise of sovereignty or sovereign rights nor such appropriation shall be recognized.
2 All rights in the resources of the Area are vested in mankind as a whole, on whose behalf the Authority shall act. These resources are not subject to alienation. The minerals recovered from the Area, however, may only be alienated in accordance with this Part and the rules, regulations and procedures of the Authority.
3 No State or natural or juridical person shall claim, acquire or exercise rights with respect to the minerals recovered from the Area except in accordance with this Part. Otherwise, no such claim, acquisition or exercise of such rights shall be recognized.

Article 138

The general conduct of States in relation to the Area shall be in accordance with the provisions of this Part, the principles embodied in the Charter of the United Nations and other rules of international law in the interests of maintaining peace and security and promoting international cooperation and mutual understanding.

Article 139

1 States Parties shall have the responsibility to ensure that activities in the Area, whether carried out by States Parties, or state enterprises or natural or juridical persons which possess the nationality of States Parties or are effectively controlled by them or their nationals, shall be carried out in conformity with this Part. The same responsibility applies to international organizations for activities in the Area carried out by such organizations.

2 Without prejudice to the rules of international law and Annex III, article 22, damage caused by the failure of a State Party or international organization to carry out its responsibilities under this Part shall entail liability; States Parties or international organizations acting together shall bear joint and several liability. A State Party shall not however be liable for damage caused by any failure to comply with this Part by a person whom it has sponsored under article 153, paragraph 2(b), if the State Party has taken all necessary and appropriate measures to secure effective compliance under article 153, paragraph 4, and Annex III, article 4, paragraph 4.

3 States Parties that are members of international organizations shall take appropriate measures to ensure the implementation of this article with respect to such organizations.

Article 140

1 Activities in the Area shall, as specifically provided for in this Part, be carried out for the benefit of mankind as a whole, irrespective of the geographical location of States, whether coastal or land-locked, and taking into particular consideration the interests and needs of developing States and of peoples who have not attained full independence or other self-governing status recognized by the United Nations in accordance with General Assembly resolution 1514 (XV) and other relevant General Assembly resolutions.

2 The Authority shall provide for the equitable sharing of financial and other economic benefits derived from activities in the Area through any appropriate mechanism, on a non-discriminatory basis, in accordance with article 160, paragraph 2(f)(i).

Article 141

The Area shall be open to use exclusively for peaceful purposes by all States, whether coastal or land-locked, without discrimination and without prejudice to the other provisions of this Part.

Article 142

1   Activities in the Area, with respect to resource deposits in the Area which lie across limits of national jurisdiction, shall be conducted with due regard to the rights and legitimate interests of any coastal State across whose jurisdiction such deposits lie.

2   Consultations, including a system of prior notification, shall be maintained with the State concerned, with a view to avoiding infringement of such rights and interests. In cases where activities in the Area may result in the exploitation of resources lying within national jurisdiction, the prior consent of the coastal State concerned shall be required.

3   Neither this Part nor any rights granted or exercised pursuant thereto shall affect the rights of coastal States to take such measures consistent with the relevant provisions of Part XII as may be necessary to prevent, mitigate or eliminate grave and imminent danger to their coastline, or related interests from pollution or threat thereof or from other hazardous occurrences resulting from or caused by any activities in the Area.

Article 143

1   Marine scientific research in the Area shall be carried out exclusively for peaceful purposes and for the benefit of mankind as a whole, in accordance with Part XIII.

2   The Authority may carry out marine scientific research concerning the Area and its resources, and may enter into contracts for that purpose. The Authority shall promote and encourage the conduct of marine scientific research in the Area, and shall coordinate and disseminate the results of such research and analysis when available.

3   States Parties may carry out marine scientific research in the Area. States Parties shall promote international cooperation in marine scientific research in the Area by:

a   participating in international programmes and encouraging cooperation in marine scientific research by personnel of different countries and of the Authority;

b   ensuring that programmes are developed through the Authority or other international organizations as appropriate for the benefit of developing States and technologically less developed States with a view to:

i   strengthening their research capabilities;

ii   training their personnel and the personnel of the Authority in the techniques and applications of research;

iii fostering the employment of their qualified personnel in research in the Area;

c   effectively disseminating the results of research and analysis when available, through the Authority or other international channels when appropriate.

Article 144

1   The Authority shall take measures in accordance with this Convention:

a   to acquire technology and scientific knowledge relating to activities in the Area; and

b   to promote and encourage the transfer to developing States of such technology and scientific knowledge so that all States Parties benefit therefrom.

2   To this end the Authority and States Parties shall cooperate in promoting the transfer of technology and scientific knowledge relating to activities in the Area so that the Enterprise and all States Parties may benefit therefrom. In particular they shall initiate and promote:

a   programmes for the transfer of technology to the Enterprise and to developing States with regard to activities in the Area, including, *inter alia*, facilitating the access of the Enterprise and of developing States to the relevant technology, under fair and reasonable terms and conditions;

b   measures directed towards the advancement of the technology of the Enterprise and the domestic technology of developing States, particularly by providing opportunities to personnel from the Enterprise and from developing States for training in marine science and technology and for their full participation in activities in the Area.

Article 145

Necessary measures shall be taken in accordance with this Convention with respect to activities in the Area to ensure effective protection for the marine environment from harmful effects which may arise from such activities. To this end the Authority shall adopt appropriate rules, regulations and procedures for *inter alia*:

a   the prevention, reduction and control of pollution and other hazards to the marine environment, including the coastline, and of interference with the ecological balance of the marine environment, particular attention being paid to the need for protection from harmful effects of such activities as drilling, dredging, excavation, disposal of waste, construction and operation or maintenance of installations, pipelines and other devices related to such activities;

b   the protection and conservation of the natural resources of the Area and the prevention of damage to the flora and fauna of the marine environment.

Article 146

With respect to activities in the Area, necessary measures shall be taken to ensure effective protection of human life. To this end the Authority shall adopt appropriate rules, regulations and procedures to supplement existing international law as embodied in relevant treaties.

Article 147

1   Activities in the Area shall be carried out with reasonable regard for other activities in the marine environment.

2   Installations used for carrying out activities in the Area shall be subject to the following conditions:

a   such installations shall be erected, emplaced and removed solely in accordance with this Part and subject to the rules, regulations and procedures of the Authority. Due notice must be given of the erection, emplacement and removal of such installations, and permanent means for giving warning of their presence must be maintained;

b   such installations may not be established where interference may be caused to the use of recognized sea lanes essential to international navigation or in areas of intense fishing activity;

c   safety zones shall be established around such installations with appropriate markings to ensure the safety of both navigation and the installations. The configuration and location of such safety zones shall not be such as to form a belt impeding the lawful access of shipping to particular maritime zones or navigation along international sea lanes;

d   such installations shall be used exclusively for peaceful purposes;

e   such installations do not possess the status of islands. They have no territorial sea of their own, and their presence does not affect the delimitation of the territorial sea, the exclusive economic zone or the continental shelf.

3   Other activities in the marine environment shall be conducted with reasonable regard for activities in the Area.

Article 148

The effective participation of developing States in activities in the Area shall be promoted as specifically provided for in this Part, having due regard to their special interests and needs, and in particular to the special need of the land-locked and geographically disadvantaged among them to overcome obstacles arising from their disadvantaged location, including remoteness from the Area and difficulty of access to and from it.

Article 149

All objects of an archaeological and historical nature found in the Area shall be preserved or disposed of for the benefit of mankind as a whole, particular regard being paid to the preferential rights of the State or country of origin, or the State of cultural origin, or the State of historical and archaeological origin (United Nations (2022). https://www.un.org/depts/los/convention_agreements/texts/unclos/closindx.htm).

Appendix B – United Nations Sustainable Development Goal Number 14: Life Below Water

14.1 By 2025, prevent and significantly reduce marine pollution of all kinds, in particular from land-based activities, including marine debris and nutrient pollution

14.2 By 2020, sustainably manage and protect marine and coastal ecosystems to avoid significant adverse impacts, including by strengthening their resilience, and take action for their restoration in order to achieve healthy and productive oceans

14.3 Minimize and address the impacts of ocean acidification, including through enhanced scientific cooperation at all levels

14.4 By 2020, effectively regulate harvesting and end overfishing, illegal, unreported and unregulated fishing and destructive fishing practices and implement science-based management plans, in order to restore fish stocks in the shortest time feasible, at least to levels that can produce maximum sustainable yield as determined by their biological characteristics

14.5 By 2020, conserve at least 10 per cent of coastal and marine areas, consistent with national and international law and based on the best available scientific information

14.6 By 2020, prohibit certain forms of fisheries subsidies which contribute to overcapacity and overfishing, eliminate subsidies that contribute to illegal, unreported and unregulated fishing and refrain from introducing new such subsidies, recognizing that appropriate and effective special and differential treatment for developing and least developed countries should be an integral part of the World Trade Organization fisheries subsidies negotiation

14.7 By 2030, increase the economic benefits to Small Island developing States and least developed countries from the sustainable use of marine resources, including through sustainable management of fisheries, aquaculture and tourism

14.A Increase scientific knowledge, develop research capacity and transfer marine technology, taking into account the Intergovernmental Oceanographic Commission Criteria and Guidelines on the Transfer of Marine Technology, in order to improve ocean health and to enhance the contribution of marine biodiversity to the development of developing countries, in particular small island developing States and least developed countries

14.B Provide access for small-scale artisanal fishers to marine resources and markets

14.C Enhance the conservation and sustainable use of oceans and their resources by implementing international law as reflected in UNCLOS, which provides the legal framework for the conservation and sustainable use of oceans and their resources, as recalled in paragraph 158 of The Future We Want (United Nations (2022). https://www.un.org/sustainabledevelopment/oceans/).

Bibliography and Further Reading

Adewuni, I. J. (2020). "African Integrated Maritime Strategy 2050: Challenges for Implementation". *Encyclopedia of Sustainable Management*. Cham, Switzerland: Springer International Publishing AG.

Afesorgbor, Sylvanus Kwaku, and Peter A. G. Van Bergeijk. (2014). "Multi-Membership and the Effectiveness of Regional Trade Agreements in Western and Southern Africa: A Comparative Study of ECOWAS and SADC". *South African Journal of Economics*, vol. 82, no. 4, pp. 518–530, doi:10.2139/ssrn.1766522.

Afesorgbor, S. K. (2013). "Revisiting the Effectiveness of African Economic Integration. A Meta-Analytic Review and Comparative Estimation Methods". Economics Working Papers No. 2013–13, Institut for Økonomi, Aarhus Universitet.

African Union (2019). *Africa Blue Economy Strategy*. Nairobi: IBAR.

African Union Commission (2016). "African Charter on Maritime Security and Safety and Development in Africa". https://au.int/en/treaties/african-charter-maritime-security-and-safety-and-development-africa-lome-charter.

African Union Commission (2012). *2050 Africa's Integrated Maritime Strategy*. Addis Ababa: AU Commission.

Alberts, E. C. (2022). "Seychelles Embraces Transparency in Fisheries, But Gaps in Data and Action Remain", Mongabay. https://news.mongabay.com.

Anderson, J. E. and E. van Wincoop (2003). "Gravity with Gravitas: A Solution to the Border Puzzle". *American Economic Review*, vol. 93 , no. 1, pp. 170–192.

Arndt, Channing and Simon J. Roberts (2018). "Key issues in regional growth and integration in Southern Africa," *Development Southern Africa*, vol. 35, no. 3.

Attri, V. N., and Narnia Bohler-Mulleris (editors) (2018). *The Blue Economy Handbook of the Indian Ocean Region*. Africa Books Collective. Johannesburg: Africa Institute of South Africa.

Attri, V. N. (2016). "*An Emerging New Development Paradigm of the Blue Economy in Indian Ocean Rim Association: A Policy Framework for the Future*". Oxford: Oxford University Press.

Attwood, C. (2013). "World's First Large Marine Ecosystem Legal Framework signed by Angola, Namibia and South Africa". Indian Ocean Rim Association (IORA), University of Mauritius.

Baier, S. L. and J. H. Bergstrand (2007). "Do Free Trade Agreements Actually Increase Members' International Trade?" *Journal of International Economics*, vol. 71 , no. 1, pp. 72–95.

Belletti, Elena and Milo McBride. (2012). "Against the Tide: Potential for Marine Renewable Energy in Western and Southern Africa". *Consilience*, no. 23, pp. 1–14.

Benkenstein, A. and R. Chevallier (2015). *Effective Governance Central to Unlocking the Potential of the Blue Economy.* Pretoria: South African Institute of International Affairs.

Bhagwati, J. and A. Panagariya (1999). "Preferential trading areas and multilateralism". In J. Bhagwati, P. Krishna, and A. Panagariya (eds), *Trading Blocs.* Cambridge, MA: MIT Press.

Biam, David J. and, Oliver C. Ruppel (2016). "Global Environment Facility". *Journal of Ocean Law and Governance in Africa*, vol. 2016, no. 1. https://www.thegef.org/newsroom/news/worlds-first-large-marine-ecosystem-legal-f ramework-signed-angola-namibia-and-south.

Bischoff, Paul-Henri. (2012). "What's been built in twenty years, SADC and Southern Africa's political and regional security culture". *Strategic Review for Southern Africa*, vol. 34, no. 2.

Brenton, P. and G. Isik (2012). *De-Fragmenting Africa: Deepening Regional Trade Integration in Goods and Services.* Washington: The World Bank.

Blane, M. and J. Sinovich (2015). "Ensuring the SADCC Maritime Interests Through Good Order at Sea". In F. Very, and T. Mandrup (eds), *Toward Good Order at Sea.* Stellenbosch: Sun Media.

Brits, Pieter and Michelle Nel. (2016). "A wake-up call for Navies in the SADC region: towards more effective maritime law enforcement", *Acta Criminologica: African Journal of Criminology & Victimology*, vol. 29, no. 2, https://hdl.handle.net/10520/EJC199485.

Bueger, C. (2017). *Concepts in Practice: The Case of the Blue Economy.* Cardiff: Cardiff University Press.

Bueger, C. and J. Stockbrugger (2016). "Pirates, Drugs and Navies", *RUSI Journal*, vol. 161, no. 5, pp. 46–52.

Bunce, Matthew (et al) (2010). "Policy Misfits, Climate Change and Cross-Scale Vulnerability in Coastal Africa: How Development Projects Undermine Resilience." *Environmental Science and Policy*, vol. 13, pp. 485–497.

Burgess, R. (2009). "The Southern African Development Community's Macroeconomic Convergence Program: Initial Performance". IMF Staff Position Note (SPN/09/14). International Monetary Fund, Washington.

Carson, Rachel (1962). *Silent Spring.* New York: Houghton and Mifflin.

Central Intelligence Agency (2017). "World Factbook". cia.gov.

Chacha, M. (2013). "Regional integration and the challenge of overlapping memberships on trade". *Journal of International Relations and Development.* http://www.palgrave.com/gp/jpurnal/41268.

Chan, C. Y. et al. (2019). "Prospects and Challenges of Fish for Food Security in Africa". *Global Food Security*, vol. 20, pp. 17–25.

Chauvin, S. & G. Gaulier (2002). "Regional Trade Integration in Southern Africa". CEPII Working Paper No. 2002–2012.

City of Cape Town (2022). "Know Your Coast". https://resource.capetown. gov.za/documentcentre/Documents/City%20research%20reports%20and%2 0review/Know_Your_Coast_2020.pdf.

Cochrane, K. L. *et al.* (2009). "Benguela Current Large Marine Ecosystem – Governance and Management for an Ecosystem Approach to Fisheries in the Region". *Coastal Management*, vol. 37, no. 3, pp. 235–254.

Colgan, Charles S. (2003). "Measurement of the Ocean and Coastal Economy: Theory and Methods". *Center for the Blue Economy, National Ocean Economics Program.*

COMESA-EAC-SADC TRIPARTITE. (2014). COMESA-EAC-SADC Tripartite. http://www.comesa-eac-sadc-tripartite.org/.

de Melo, Jaime, & Yvonne Tsikata, (2014). "Regional Integration in Africa". *WIDER Working Paper 2014/037.* Helsinki, Finland: World Institute for Development Economics Research.

Devine, J. D. (1994). "Marine developments in Southern Africa". *Ocean & Coastal Management*, vol. 22, no. 1, pp. 89–97.

Doidge, Mathew (2007). "Joined at the hip: Regionalism and Inter-regionalism". *Journal of European Integration*, vol. 29, no. 2.

Doyle, T. (2018). "Blue Economy in the Indian Ocean Rim". *Journal of the Indian Ocean Region*, vol. 14, no. 1, pp. 1–6.

Dosenrode, Soren (ed.). (2015). *Limits to Regional Integration.* Burlington, VT: Ashgate Publishing. Limited.

Draper, Peter. (2010). "Rethinking the (European) Foundations of Sub-Saharan African Regional Economic Integration". *OECD Development Centre Working Papers No. 293.* Paris, France: OECD Publishing.

Economic Commission for Africa. (2012). *"Regional Integration in Africa (ARIA V): Towards an African Continental Free Trade Area.* Addis Ababa: Economic Commission for Africa.

Economist Intelligence Unit (2015). *Investing in the Blue Economy: Growth Opportunities on a Sustainable Ocean Economy.* London: Economist Intelligence Unit.

Edmond, Patrick, Kristof Titeca and Erik Kennes (2019). "The DRC–Angola Offshore Oil Dispute: *How Regime (In)Security Outweighs Sovereign Claims"*, vol. 45, no. 5.

Fioramonti, Lorenzo and Mattheis Frank (2015). "Is Africa Really Following Europe? An Integrated Framework for Comparative Regionalism". *JCMS Journal of Common Market Studies.*

Francis, Julius, Agneta Nilsson and Dixon Waruinge (2022). "Marine Protected Areas in the Eastern African Region: How Successful Are They?" *BioOne Complete*, vol. 31, no. 7–8, pp. 503–511.

Geta, A. & H. Kibret (2002). "Regional Economic Integration in Africa: A Review of Problems and Prospects with a Case Study of COMESA". (Working Paper). Addis Ababa University. Department of Economics, Addis Ababa, Ethiopia.

Gibb, Richard. (2012). "The Southern African Customs Union: Promoting Stability through Dependence." In *Region-building in Southern Africa: Progress, Problems and Prospects*, edited by Chris Saunders, Gwinyayi A. Dzinesa, and Dawn Nagar, London: Zed Books, pp. 148–164.

Grey, E. (2018). "Can Landlocked Countries develop a Blue Economy?", *Ship Technology*, 29 January.

Gunning, J. (2001). "Trade blocs: Relevant for Africa?", *Journal of African Economies*, vol. 10, no. 3.

Hartzenberg, Trudi. (2011). "Regional Integration in Africa". *International Journal of Economy, Management and Social Sciences*, vol. 2, no. 5, pp. 133–155.

Hosny, Amr Sadek. (2013). Theories of Economic Integration: A Survey of the Economic and Political Literature. *International Journal of Economy, Management and Social Sciences*, vol. 2, no. 5, pp. 133–135.

Indian Ocean Rim Association (2015). "Mauritius Declaration on Blue Economy". iora-mauritius-declaration-on-blue-economy.pdf.

ISS (2018). "Southern Africa Report". No. 14. https://hdl.handle.net/10520/EJC-1486da2c5c.

Jensen, H. G. and R. Sandrey (2011). "The tripartite Free Trade Agreement: A computer analysis of the impacts". *Tralac Working Paper No. IIWP06/2011*, Stellenbosch: Tralac.

Kahiri, B. and F. K. Masjidi (2012). "Landlocked Countries: A Way to Integrate with Coastal Economies". *Journal of Economic Integration*, vol. 27, no. 4, pp. 505–519.

Kelegama, Saman (1998). "Can Open Regionalism Work in the Indian Ocean Rim Association for Regional Co-operation?". *ASEAN Economic Research Bulletin*, pp. 135–167.

Laris, Joris, et al (2017). "Blue Growth and Sustainable in Indian Ocean Governance". *The Hague Institute for Global Justice Policy Brief*. http://www.thehagueinstituteforglobaljustice.org/wp-content/uploads/2017.

Larson, J. (2015). "Towards Maritime Strategy in the Indian Ocean: The Case of Seychelles". *Island Studies: Indian Ocean*, vol. 3, pp. 50–57.

Lathtop, C. (2011). "Continental Shelf Delimitation Beyond 200 Nautical Miles: Approaches Taken by Coastal States Before the Commission on the Limits of the Continental Shelf". In Colson, D. A. and R. W. Smith (eds), *International Maritime Boundaries*.

Llewellyn, L., English, S. and Barnwell, S. (2016). "A Roadmap to a Sustainable Indian Ocean Blue Economy". *Journal of the Indian Ocean Region*, no. 12, pp. 52–66.

Magliveras, Konstantinos D. (2007). "The Southern African Development Community: The Organisation, Its Policies and Prospects". *International Organizations Law Review*, vol. 4, no. 1.

Mohanty, S. L. et al. (2015). *Prospects of Blue Economy in the Indian Ocean.* New Delhi: Research and Information System for Developing Countries.

Monnererau, L. and Failler, P. (2014). *Unlocking the Fill Potential of the Blue Economy: Are African Small Island Developing States Ready to Embrace the Opportunities?* African Climate Policy Center and Economic Commission for Africa.

Moyo. T. (2017). *Promoting Inclusive and Sustainable Industrialization in Africa: A review of Progress, Challenges and Prospects.* South Africa: University of Limpopo.

Nagar, Dawn. (2012). "Regional Economic Integration." In Chris Saunders, Gwinyayi A. Dzinesa, and Dawn Nagar (eds), *Region-building in Southern Africa: Progress, Problems and Prospects*, London: Zed Books, pp.131–148.

Nel, Michelle and Francois Vrey. (2016). "Africa's Rising Maritime Agenda: Public Goods at Sea" *Acta Criminologica: African Journal of Criminology and Victimology*, vol. 29, no. 1, pp. 156–17001.

Onditi, Francis and Douglas Yates (2012). *Illusions of Location Theory: Consequences for Blue Economy in Africa.* New York: Version Press.

Organization for Economic Cooperation and Development (2016). *The Ocean Economy in 2030.* Paris: OECD.

Pauli, Gunter (2017). *The Blue Economy.* London: Paradigm Press.

Pauli, Gunter (2010). *The Blue Economy 3.0.* New York: XLIBRIS.

Potgieter, T. D. (2012). "Maritime Security in the Indian Ocean: Strategic Setting and Features", https://hdl.handle.net/10520/EJC125404.

Potgieter, T. D. (2018). "Oceans Economy, Blue Economy and Security: Notes on the South African Potential and developments." *Journal of the Indian Ocean Region*, vol. 14, pp. 49–70.

Potgieter T. and T. Walker, (2015). "The 2050 African Integrated Maritime Strategy: Content and Progress". In F. Very, and T. Mandrup (eds), *Toward Good Order at Sea.* Stellenbosch: Sun Media.

Rembe, N. S. (1980). *Africa and the International Law of the Sea: Study of the Contribution of the African States to the Third UN Conference on the Law of the Sea.* Alphen aan den Rijn: Sljhoff and Noordhoff.

Roa, P. V. (2014). "Managing Africa's Maritime Domain: Issues and Challenges". *Journal of the Indian Ocean Region*, vol. 10, pp. 113–123.

Royeppen, A. and F. A. Kornegay (2015). *Southern African and the Indian Ocean-South Atlantic Nexus: Blue Economy and Prospects for Regional Cooperation.* Pretoria: South Africa Institute for Global Dialogue.

Roy, Aparana (2019). "Blue Economy in the Indian Ocean: Governance Perspectives for Sustainable Development in the Region". *ORF Occasional Paper*, 181.

SADC. (2015b). *SADC Industrialization Strategy and Road Map.* SADC Secretariat, Gaborone.

SADC. (2012). *Regional Infrastructure Development Master Plan*. SADC Secretariat, Gaborone.

SADC. (2015a). *SADC Success Stories (Volume 1)*. SADC Secretariat, Gaborone.

Sahuque, Raymond (2015). "The Blue Economy: Progress on the Development of the Blue Economy in Seychelles. Ministry of Finance, Trade, and the Blue Economy". June. https://wedocs.unep.org/bitstream/handle/20.500. 11822/21092/Blue%20Economy_presentation_16%20June%202015_FF.pdf? sequence=1&isAllowed=y.

Soko, Mills (2007). "The political economy of regional integration in Southern Africa". *Notre Europe*, vol. 23.

Sparks, D. L. (2018). "The Southern African Development Community: Toward a Deeper and Wider Union?" in Looney, Robert (ed), *The Handbook of International Trade Agreements: World Integration or Division?* London: Taylor and Francis Group, pp. 359–372.

Sparks, D. L. (1985). *Marine Resources as a Base for Industrial Development: Problems and Prospects in The Western Indian Ocean Island States*. Consultant Report (Principle author). Vienna: United Nations Industrial Development Organization.

Sparks, D. L. (1984). *Final Report: Regional Workshop for Coastal and Marine Management and Protection in East Africa and the Indian Ocean*. Charleston, SC: South Carolina Sea Grant Consortium/International Union for Conservation of Nature and Natural Resources.

Sparks, D. L. (1984). *Programme for Action: Report on a Management Strategy for the Conservation and Development of Coastal and Marine Resources in East Africa and the Indian Ocean Region* (edited, with James Dobbin and Dan Finn), Charleston, SC: South Carolina Sea Grant Consortium/International Union for Conservation of Nature and Natural Resources.

Sparks, D. L. (2016). "The Sustainable Development Goals and Agenda 2063: Implications for Economic Integration in Africa". *Research in Applied Economics*, vol. 8, no. 4, pp.12–40.

Sparks, D. L. (1986) "Marine Resources Development Potential in the Western Indian Ocean Island States". *Central Bank of Seychelles Quarterly Review*, November(serialized in *Seychelles Nation*, November 26, 1986, December 3, 1986, December 10, 1986, December 17, 1986, December 24, 1986, January 7, 1987, January 14, 1987).

Sparks, D. L. (1996). "Mining Sector and Environmental Conservation in Namibia: Providing Lessons for the Region". Paper presented to the African Studies Association and Canadian Studies Association annual meeting, Toronto, Canada, November, 1994; to the Office of Economic Analysis, Department of State, Washington, DC May 1995; and, to the Economics Association of Swaziland, October.

Sparks, D. L. (1989). "Prospects for Namibia's Fisheries and Marine Resources". Paper presented to the United Nations Council for Namibia's

"Seminar on the Integration of Namibia into Regional Structures for Economic Co-operation and Development in Southern Africa", Harare, Zimbabwe.

Sparks, D. L. (1988). "Economic Development in Small Island Economies: Marine Resources and Appropriate Technology in the Indian Ocean". Paper presented to "Islands '88: Conference of the Islands of the World", Hobart, Tasmania: University of Tasmania.

Sparks, D. L. (1987). "Seychelles, Mauritius, Maldives and Comoros: Problems and Prospects for Small Island Economies". Paper presented in absentia to the African Studies Association Annual Meeting, Denver, Colorado.

Sparks, D. L. (1982). "Namibia's Coastal and Marine Resources Development". Paper presented to the University of Vermont's conference, "Namibia, Africa's Last Colony: Problems for Freedom and Development", Burlington, Vermont.

Sparks, D. L. (1979). "Walvis Bay, Plumpudding and Penguin Islands: Their History and Economic Importance to Namibia." Paper presented to the African Studies Association annual meeting, Los Angeles, California.

Sparks, D. L (ed.) (2021). *The Blue Economy in Sub-Saharan Africa*. London: RoutledgePress, Taylor & Francis Group.

Sparks, D. L. (2022). "Code Red for Africa's Blue Economy". *African Arguments*, 24 March.

Surbun, Vishal (2021). "Africa's combined exclusive maritime zone concept". *ISS Africa Report Institute for Security Studies Papers*, Vol. 2012, No. 236. https://hdl.handle.net/10520/ejc-isafrica-v2020-n32-a1.

Swanepoel. Ernesta. (2020). "The Law of the Sea and Landlocked States". *Policy Brief, South African Institute for international Affairs*.

Tonazzini, D. et al (2019). *Blue Tourism: Toward a Sustainable Coastal and Marine Tourism in World Marine Regions*. Barcelona: Eco-Union.

United Nations Conference on Trade and Development (2014). *The Oceans Economy: Opportunities and Challenges for Small Island Developing States*. Geneva: UNCTAD.

United Nations Convention on the Law of the Sea (1982). *Montego Bay*, 10 December. legal.un.org/avl//pdf/ha/uncls/uncls_e.pdf.

United Nations Economic Commission for Africa (2016). *Africa's Blue Economy: A Policy Handbook*. Addis Ababa: UNECA.

United Nations Economic Commission for Africa (2020). *Blue Economy, Inclusive Industrialization and Economic Development in Southern Africa*. Addis Ababa: UNECA.

United Nations Environment Programme (2015). *Blue Economy: Sharing Success Stories to Inspire Change*. Nairobi:UNEP.

United Nations Food and Agriculture Organization (2018). *The State of the World Fisheries and Aquaculture: Meeting the Sustainable Development Goals*. Rome: FAO.

United Nations Food and Agriculture Organization (2022). *Fishery and Aquaculture Country Profiles*. Rome: FAO.

VanderZwaag, D. (2008). "Overview if regional Cooperation in Coastal and Oceans Governance". In C. Thai-Eng, et al (eds), *Securing the Oceans: Essays on Ocean Governance – Global and Regional Perspectives*. Quezon City: GEF/UNDP/IMO.

Vanheukelom, Jan and Talitha Bertelsmann-Scott (2016). *The Political Economy of Regional Integration in Africa: The Southern African Development Community (SADC)*. Maastricht: ECDPM.

Van Wyk, J. (2016). "Defining the Blue Economy as a South African Strategy Priority: Towards a Sustainable 10ᵗʰ Province?" *Journal of the Indian Ocean Region*, Vol. 11, pp. 153–169.

Vousden, D. et al. (2008). "Establishing a Basis for Ecosystem Management in the Western Indian Ocean". *South African Journal of Science*, vol. 104, no. 11, pp. 417–420.

Vrancken, P. H. G. (2018). "The African Perspective in Global Ocean Governance". In D. Attard, D. Ong, and D. Kristsiotis (eds). *The IMLI Treatise on Global Ocean Governance*. Oxford: Oxford University Press.

Vrancken, P. H. G and M. K. Tsamenyl (eds) (2017). *The Law of the Sea: The African Union and Its Member States*. Cape Town: Juta.

Vrancken, P. H. G. (2020). "The 2050 African Integrated Maritime Strategy: The Combined Exclusive Zone of Africa as an Instrument of Sustainable Development of the African Large Marine Ecosystems". *Environmental Development*.

Walker, Timothy (2018). "Securing a sustainable oceans economy: South Africa's Approach". https://hdl.handle.net/10520/EJC-1486da2c5c.

World Bank (2017). *The Potential of the Blue Economy: Increased Long-Term benefits of the Sustainable Use of Marine Resources for Small Island Developing States and Coastal Least Developed Countries*. Washington, DC: IBRD.

World Bank (2016). *Blue Economy Development Framework: Growing the Blue Economy to Combat Poverty and Accelerate Prosperity*. Washington: International Bank for Reconstruction and Development.

Zyuulu, I. (2010). "Convergence in the SADC and African Economic Integration Process: Prospects". *IFC Bulletin*, vol. 32, pp. 96–105.

Index

Abidjan Convention 39–40
Africa Integrated Maritime Strategy (AIMS 2050) 4; major issues for 5; strategic actions planned 6
African Caribbean and Pacific (ACP) group 14–15
African Development Bank (ADB) 36
African Union (AU) 5, 37; Africa Integrated Maritime Strategy (AIMS 2050) 4, 5; African Charter on Maritime Security and Safety and Development (Lome Charter, 2016) 6; Agenda 2063 initiative 6; Policy Framework and Reform Strategy for Fisheries and Aquaculture in Africa (2014) 6
Air Mauritius 14
Angola 20; Abidjan Convention, party to 39–40; blue resources, dilemma regarding 20; Cabinda enclave, oil in 20; environmental, social, and governance (ESG) standards, balance in 43; Environmental Framework Act in 43; Exclusive Economic Zone (EEZ) of 13; exports/imports (2000 and 2015) 28; Joint Interest Zone (JIZ) with DRC 20; off-shore mining 43; oil, most valuable resource for 20; oil, production and exploration of 43
Anjouan, deep-water port at 20

aquaculture: in Madagascar 22; in Mozambique 21; in Namibia 40; in Namibia, funding for 17; in South Africa 19
artisanal fisheries in Mozambique 41–2
artisanal industry in Comoros 44

Bazaruto Archipelago National Park in Mozambique 10
Benguela Current 2, 18, 31; fishing from Namibia in 17
biodiversity 10
biological diversity of areas beyond national jurisdiction (BBNJ) 13
Blue Bond financing, Seychelles and 16–17, 41
The Blue Economy (Pauli, G.) 3
Blue Economy Coordinating Unit (SADC-BECU) 37–8, 39, 45–6
blue economy in South Africa 18
Blue Economy Roadmap (2018) in Seychelles 15
blue resources: Comoros dependence on 19; dilemma in Angola and DRC regarding 20
Botswana 13, 24, 26, 30, 45; exports/imports (2000 and 2015) 28

Cabinda enclave, oil in 20
Carson, Rachel 3
CBD Sustainable Oceans Initiative 38
China, People's Republic of 16

For Product Safety Concerns and Information please contact our EU
representative GPSR@taylorandfrancis.com
Taylor & Francis Verlag GmbH, Kaufingerstraße 24, 80331 München, Germany

www.ingramcontent.com/pod-product-compliance
Ingram Content Group UK Ltd.
Pitfield, Milton Keynes, MK11 3LW, UK
UKHW021420080625
459435UK00011B/95